BIOECONOMY AND ENTREPRENEURSHIP

K VALARMATHY
P.TAMIZHARASI

Made with ♥ on the Notion Press Platform
www.notionpress.com

"To my beloved mother, husband, and daughter: This book is a testament to your unwavering support, love, and inspiration. Thank you for being my pillars of strength and the heart of every word written here."

Contents

PREFACE

In recent years, the intersection of biological resources and economic development has given rise to the concept of the bioeconomy. As global challenges such as climate change, resource scarcity, and environmental degradation continue to grow, bioeconomy offers a sustainable approach to innovation and economic progress. This book, Bioeconomy and Entrepreneurship, explores how entrepreneurial ventures can harness biological resources to create sustainable solutions and drive economic growth.

Through real-world examples, research insights, and practical frameworks, this book aims to provide readers with a comprehensive understanding of how bioeconomy principles can foster resilient businesses and sustainable ecosystems.

ACKNOWLEDGEMENTS

I extend my deepest gratitude to those who have supported and inspired me throughout the creation of this book. My sincere thanks to Dr. S.N.V.L. Narasimha Raju, President and Chairman of The Oxford Educational Institutions, for his visionary guidance and unwavering support. I am also grateful to Dr. H.N. Ramesh, Principal, and Dr. B.K. Manjunath, Head of the Biotechnology Department, for their encouragement and invaluable insights.

Heartfelt thanks to my mother, P. Pushpavathy, whose strength has been my foundation; my husband, T. Lakshmikanth, for his steadfast support; and my daughter, L. Siaahni, who brings joy and purpose to my life. I am equally grateful to my friends and colleagues, whose camaraderie and motivation have been instrumental in this journey.

I

INTRODUCTION

Bio-economics

Bio-economics blends principles of biology and economics, focusing on managing and conserving biological resources within economic systems. It examines how biological systems, from ecosystems to individual species, can be maintained sustainably as essential components of the economy.

Concept of Bio-economics

The core of bio-economics lies in balancing economic growth with the sustainable use of biological resources. Unlike traditional economics, which often treats resources as infinite, bio-economics considers the finite nature of these resources, factoring in the ecological limits of regeneration and environmental impacts. It emphasizes the need to manage resources like forests, fish stocks, water, and agricultural biodiversity responsibly to ensure both ecological and economic sustainability.

Development of Economics and Bioscience

As economic growth pressures natural resources, biosciences play a crucial role in understanding ecosystems, resource regeneration rates, and biodiversity's role in economic productivity. Bio-economics has emerged as a field to address how economies can adapt to maintain environmental balance. Key developments include sustainable farming practices, renewable energy sources, and conservation policies informed by ecological science.

Resource Economics and Scarcity of Biological Resources

Resource economics within bio-economics addresses how to manage scarcity in biological resources by creating policies that incentivize conservation and sustainable use. As these resources become limited, the economic models prioritize not just their use but their long-term preservation. This scarcity-driven approach integrates the ecological cost of resource depletion, offering tools like carbon credits, quotas, and sustainable harvest models to mitigate over-exploitation.

Through bio-economics, the goal is to achieve a sustainable economy that thrives in harmony with nature's capacity, safeguarding biodiversity while fostering economic resilience.

Bioresource Elasticity

Bioresource Elasticity measures how the demand or supply of biological resources responds to changes in their availability or in external economic factors like price, income, or environmental shifts. This concept, adapted from traditional elasticity in economics, helps assess how sensitive natural resources are to exploitation pressures and environmental changes, offering insight into sustainable management practices.

Key Aspects of Bioresource Elasticity

Supply Elasticity of Bioresources: This assesses how much the availability or harvest of a biological resource (e.g., timber, fish stocks) responds to changes in market prices or other economic factors. For example, if fish prices rise, a highly elastic resource would see an increase in fishing activity. However, biological resources typically have lower elasticity since they are bound by ecological constraints like reproduction rates and seasonal availability.

Demand Elasticity of Bioresources: This evaluates how consumer demand for a resource reacts to price or income changes. If a resource is inelastic in demand, price hikes may not significantly decrease demand (e.g., staple foods). In contrast, demand for elastic resources (e.g., luxury goods derived from rare species) may drop significantly with price increases, helping reduce exploitation pressures.

Ecological Constraints and Regeneration Rates: Biological resources, unlike manufactured goods, depend on natural growth cycles and environmental conditions. The regenerative capacity of ecosystems limits the elasticity of these resources. For instance, forests or fish populations cannot instantly respond to increased demand because their growth and replenishment are gradual, constrained by ecological limits.

Implications for Sustainable Management: Understanding bioresource elasticity aids in setting sustainable harvest levels, regulating market access, and designing conservation policies. If a resource is inelastic, policy-makers may need stricter controls to prevent overuse. For elastic resources, incentives and demand management might be more effective.

Applications in Bio-economics

Bioresource elasticity is essential in bio-economics, informing resource management and economic policy. By analyzing how resources react to changes in economic conditions, bio-economists can predict over-exploitation risks and design policies that promote conservation. This approach helps in maintaining an ecological-economic balance, ensuring that bioresources remain available for future use while supporting current economic needs.

Evolution and Development of Economics and Biology (Charles Darwin and the evolutionary paradigm)

The evolution and development of economics and biology have long been interlinked, particularly through the influence of evolutionary theory pioneered by Charles Darwin. Darwin's work on evolution, especially his theory of natural selection, transformed biological sciences and inspired economists to explore analogous principles in understanding human behavior, markets, and resource allocation.

Darwin's Influence: The Evolutionary Paradigm

Charles Darwin's On the Origin of Species (1859) introduced the idea that species evolve over time through natural selection, where organisms better adapted to their environments have higher chances of survival and reproduction. This evolutionary paradigm presented a new way of understanding change, competition, adaptation, and survival. In biology, it shifted the focus from static classifications to dynamic processes that shape life over time.

In economics, Darwin's theory inspired the concept that economic systems, like biological ecosystems, are adaptive and subject to evolutionary forces. Economists began to view markets as environments where businesses "compete" for survival, and those better able to adapt to changes in technology, consumer preferences, or resources are more likely to thrive.

Evolutionary Economics: The Development of Economic Thought

In the early 20th century, economists such as Thorstein Veblen introduced concepts that directly connected Darwinian ideas to economic theories. Veblen argued that human behavior, just like biological traits, could evolve over time based on adaptive needs, shaping habits, preferences, and social structures. Later, economists used evolutionary principles to explain complex market behaviors, including how industries adapt, how firms innovate, and how consumer habits evolve.

Adaptive Efficiency and Competition: Economists recognized that firms and industries exhibit adaptive efficiency, where businesses must continuously innovate and adapt to survive market changes, similar to organisms adapting to environmental pressures.

Cumulative Development: Evolutionary economics posits that economic development is cumulative. Innovations, once introduced, build on previous advances, much like biological evolution where new traits accumulate over generations. This cumulative aspect explains why economic growth often follows a pattern of small, incremental improvements rather than sudden leaps.

Survival of the Fittest and Market Selection: Darwin's "survival of the fittest" principle aligns with the market selection concept in economics. Firms that efficiently use resources, meet consumer demand, and innovate are more likely to survive, while others may exit the market. This market-driven competition for survival parallels natural selection.

Evolutionary Development in Biology and Economics

The parallel development of evolutionary biology and economics helped create the interdisciplinary fields of bio-economics and evolutionary economics, both of which study how adaptive processes shape both biological and economic systems.

In biology, evolution explains species diversity, adaptation to habitats, and genetic changes over time. In economics, the evolutionary approach explains how market structures emerge, how companies grow and decline, and how economic systems adapt to new challenges like technological disruptions or environmental limits.

Modern Applications of the Evolutionary Paradigm

Today, evolutionary concepts are widely used to address global challenges, such as sustainable resource management, environmental protection, and economic resilience. By applying adaptive principles, economists and biologists work together to:

Promote Sustainable Practices: Evolutionary theories support sustainable practices by emphasizing long-term adaptation over short-term exploitation, as seen in conservation biology and resource economics.

Encourage Innovation: Understanding adaptation in both fields leads to fostering innovation, where economies and ecosystems both benefit from diverse, adaptable solutions.

Design Resilient Systems: Evolutionary principles help design systems that are resilient to change, whether through biodiversity preservation or creating diversified, adaptive economies.

In summary, Darwin's evolutionary paradigm has been foundational in developing both biology and economics. It introduced adaptive principles that not only transformed our understanding of life but also reshaped economic thought, allowing both fields to evolve with a focus on sustainability, resilience, and long-term adaptation.

Introduction to Bio-Business in the Indian Context

Bio-business encompasses industries that utilize biological systems, organisms, or derivatives to create products and services. In India, the bio-business sector has rapidly grown due to advancements in biotechnology, agricultural sciences, healthcare, and environmental sustainability. India's bio-economy is driven by agricultural innovation, bio-pharmaceuticals, biofuels, and bioinformatics, supported by government initiatives like Make in India and the National Biotechnology Development Strategy. India's vast biodiversity, skilled workforce, and growing market for sustainable products make it an ideal environment for bio-business growth.

SWOT Analysis of Bio-Business in India

Strengths

Diverse Biodiversity: India's rich biodiversity provides a wide variety of raw materials, making it an ideal location for developing bio-based products.

Skilled Workforce: A large pool of scientists, researchers, and skilled labor trained in biotechnology and life sciences.

Government Support: Policies like the Biotechnology Industry Research Assistance Council (BIRAC) and initiatives to foster startups enhance the growth environment for bio-business.

Growing Market Demand: Rising health awareness and demand for sustainable, eco-friendly products are fueling growth in bio-products like organic foods, biofuels, and natural healthcare products.

Weaknesses

High R&D Costs: Bio-businesses require significant investment in research and development, which can be challenging for small and medium enterprises (SMEs) to afford.

Regulatory Challenges: Complex regulatory frameworks and long approval timelines can delay product launches, especially in pharmaceuticals and biotechnology.

Limited Infrastructure: Lack of high-quality research infrastructure in rural and semi-urban areas can limit accessibility for startups and smaller companies.

Dependency on Imports: Many bio-businesses still rely on imported technology and raw materials, which increases operational costs.

Opportunities

Sustainable Development Goals (SDGs): Growing emphasis on sustainability aligns with bio-business products, offering potential for bio-businesses focused on waste management, renewable resources, and green technologies.

Export Potential: India's bio-business sector has a strong potential for export, especially in bio-pharmaceuticals, organic products, and herbal health supplements.

Investment in Rural Bio-business: Integrating bio-business into rural India could increase employment, promote sustainable agricultural practices, and enhance the rural economy.

Collaborations and Partnerships: Opportunities for collaboration with international firms in biotech, agri-tech, and renewable energy sectors can bring in expertise, technology, and investment.

Threats

Market Competition: Intense competition from global bio-business leaders, especially in high-tech areas like bio-pharmaceuticals and genetic research, poses challenges.

Intellectual Property (IP) Issues: Bio-businesses are often at risk of IP disputes and challenges, especially in biotechnology and pharmaceutical innovations.

Environmental and Ethical Concerns: Bio-business activities, especially genetically modified organisms (GMOs) and biopharmaceuticals, may face opposition due to ethical, environmental, or health concerns.

Economic Instability: Fluctuations in currency value, trade policies, and economic slowdowns can affect bio-businesses that rely on global supply chains and exports.

Ownership and Development of Entrepreneurship

Entrepreneurship involves creating, developing, and managing a new business venture to generate profit and achieve growth. Ownership, which includes sole proprietorships, partnerships, and corporations, defines the legal structure and the distribution of responsibilities and profits. Development of entrepreneurship includes skill-building, funding access, and strategic planning, which are essential for establishing and scaling new ventures.

Stages in the Entrepreneurial Process

Idea Generation: Identifying a business opportunity based on market needs, personal interest, or unique insights.

Feasibility Analysis: Conducting market, technical, financial, and social feasibility studies to assess the viability of the idea.

Planning: Creating a business plan that outlines objectives, strategies, and the path to profitability.

Resource Gathering: Securing funding, building a team, and acquiring other essential resources.

Implementation: Launching the business, establishing operations, and refining the product or service.

Growth and Expansion: Scaling the business by increasing market reach, diversifying products, and enhancing operational efficiency.

Role of Entrepreneurs in Economic Development

Entrepreneurs drive economic development by creating jobs, fostering innovation, and improving productivity. They stimulate economic activity, contribute to GDP, and introduce new products or technologies. Entrepreneurs also promote competition, which enhances quality and decreases prices, and they contribute to community development by providing employment and supporting local supply chains.

Entrepreneurship in India

India has seen rapid growth in entrepreneurship, particularly in technology, e-commerce, and bio-based industries. Government programs like Startup India and financial support from initiatives like the Micro Units Development and Refinance Agency (MUDRA) have encouraged entrepreneurship. India's young demographic, extensive digital adoption, and growing investment ecosystem support a vibrant entrepreneurial landscape.

Barriers to Entrepreneurship

Financial Constraints: Limited access to funding or high-interest rates can restrict startup growth.

Regulatory Challenges: Complex regulations and bureaucratic processes create hurdles, especially for small businesses.

Market Competition: Intense competition from larger, established firms can deter small startups.

Lack of Infrastructure: Poor infrastructure, particularly in rural areas, hinders the setup and scale of businesses.

Skill Gaps: Limited access to skill-building resources and mentorship affects entrepreneurship development.

Small Scale Industries (SSIs)

Definition: Small Scale Industries (SSIs) are businesses with limited capital investment, smaller workforce, and lower production capacity, focusing on local markets and niche products.

Characteristics:

Limited capital investment and workforce

Local resource utilization and tailored market offerings

Focus on labor-intensive production and less automated processes

Need and Rationale:

SSIs contribute to job creation, regional development, and economic diversification. They help reduce regional imbalances and empower communities by creating local employment.

Objectives:

Promote balanced economic development

Generate employment opportunities

Foster self-reliance and reduce dependence on imports

Encourage innovation and entrepreneurship in rural areas

Scope: SSIs span various sectors, including manufacturing, textiles, agriculture, and services, with a particular focus on supporting rural industries.

Feasibility Studies

Market Feasibility Study: Examines demand, competition, customer preferences, and potential market size.

Technical Feasibility Study: Assesses the technical requirements, availability of technology, and resources needed.

Financial Feasibility Study: Analyzes costs, potential revenue, funding requirements, and profitability.

Social Feasibility Study: Evaluates the societal impact, community acceptance, and alignment with social values and norms.

Global Bio-Business and Industry Future Trends

The bio-business industry globally is poised for growth, driven by advances in biotechnology, healthcare, and sustainability. Future trends include:

Increased Biofuel Production: To reduce carbon emissions, biofuels and renewable energy are gaining traction.

Personalized Medicine: Biopharmaceuticals and genetic engineering are advancing precision medicine.

Agri-Tech Growth: Sustainable farming solutions, like bio-fertilizers and gene-edited crops, are addressing food security.

Circular Bioeconomy: Emphasis on waste recycling and bio-based products to create a sustainable, regenerative economic model.

These trends highlight bio-business as a vital driver for sustainable economic development and innovation in the global economy.

II

BIOECONOMY

Benefits of a Knowledge-Based Bioeconomy

A knowledge-based bioeconomy refers to the integration of biotechnology, life sciences, and knowledge-intensive practices in various sectors to produce sustainable products, processes, and services. This approach leverages scientific research and innovation to optimize the use of biological resources. Here are the detailed benefits:

Sustainable Resource Utilization:

Renewable Resources: A bioeconomy emphasizes the use of renewable biological resources, which helps reduce reliance on fossil fuels and promotes sustainability.

Waste Reduction: By utilizing agricultural, forestry, and industrial waste as feedstock, bioeconomy practices minimize waste and enhance resource efficiency.

Economic Growth and Job Creation:

New Markets and Industries: The bioeconomy fosters the development of new sectors, such as biofuels, bioplastics, and pharmaceuticals, contributing to economic diversification.

Employment Opportunities: Knowledge-based bioeconomy creates high-skill jobs in research, development, production, and management, leading to enhanced employment opportunities.

Innovation and Technological Advancement:

Research and Development (R&D): Investment in biotechnology and life sciences drives innovation, leading to the development of new products and technologies that improve productivity and sustainability.

Knowledge Transfer: Collaborative efforts between academia, industry, and government facilitate knowledge sharing, accelerating the translation of research into practical applications.

Environmental Benefits:

Reduced Carbon Footprint: Bio-based products and processes typically have a lower environmental impact, contributing to climate change mitigation.

Biodiversity Preservation: Sustainable practices promote the conservation of biodiversity by maintaining healthy ecosystems and reducing habitat destruction.

Enhanced Food Security:

Improved Agricultural Practices: The bioeconomy supports the development of genetically modified organisms (GMOs) and other innovative agricultural technologies that increase crop yields and resilience to climate change.

Sustainable Food Production: Bioeconomy initiatives can lead to the production of safer, healthier food products that are more efficient to produce.

Social Benefits:

Community Engagement: Knowledge-based bioeconomy initiatives often involve local communities in the sustainable management of resources, promoting social equity and empowerment.

Health Improvements: Innovations in biotechnology contribute to the development of new medicines and healthcare solutions, enhancing public health outcomes.

Challenges of a Knowledge-Based Bioeconomy

While the knowledge-based bioeconomy presents numerous advantages, several challenges must be addressed to realize its full potential:

High Research and Development Costs:

Financial Barriers: Developing bio-based technologies requires substantial investments in R&D, which can be a barrier for small and medium enterprises (SMEs) and startups.

Long Development Times: The time needed to develop, test, and commercialize new bio-based products can be lengthy, delaying potential returns on investment.

Regulatory Hurdles:

Complex Approval Processes: Navigating regulatory frameworks for biotechnology can be challenging, with lengthy approval processes that can hinder innovation.

Uncertainty in Regulations: Changing regulations and lack of clarity regarding biotechnology can create uncertainty for businesses, discouraging investment.

Public Acceptance and Ethical Concerns:

Skepticism towards GMOs: Many consumers are wary of genetically modified organisms and bio-based products, necessitating public education and transparent communication about their benefits.

Ethical Issues: Concerns about the ethical implications of biotechnology, such as gene editing, may lead to public resistance and regulatory constraints.

Market Competition:

Established Industries: Competing with traditional industries that rely on fossil fuels and conventional practices can be difficult for emerging bio-based sectors.

Price Competitiveness: Bio-based products may initially have higher costs than their conventional counterparts, making market penetration challenging.

Resource Competition:

Land and Water Use: Increased demand for biomass may lead to competition for agricultural land and water resources, potentially impacting food security.

Ecological Impact: Unsustainable harvesting of biological resources can harm ecosystems and biodiversity if not properly managed.

Knowledge Gaps and Skills Shortages:

Workforce Development: There is a need for skilled professionals trained in biotechnology and related fields. A shortage of qualified personnel can hinder the growth of the bioeconomy.

Research Gaps: Continued investment in R&D is necessary to address knowledge gaps and develop innovative solutions that meet market needs.

Sustainable Food Security: Europe and Africa Perspectives

Sustainable food security is a multifaceted issue that involves ensuring all people have access to sufficient, safe, and nutritious food to meet their dietary needs while promoting sustainable agricultural practices that do not deplete natural resources. Here's a detailed look at how this concept manifests in Europe and Africa.

Sustainable Food Security in Europe

1. Policy Frameworks and Initiatives

Common Agricultural Policy (CAP): The European Union (EU) has implemented CAP to support farmers, promote sustainable practices, and ensure food security. CAP encourages environmentally friendly farming practices, crop rotation, and organic farming, thus enhancing soil health and biodiversity.

Farm to Fork Strategy: Aimed at making food systems fair, healthy, and environmentally-friendly, this strategy seeks to reduce the environmental and climate footprint of food production. It focuses on sustainable practices and encourages a shift towards plant-based diets.

2. Agricultural Practices

Sustainable Intensification: This approach seeks to increase food production while minimizing environmental impact. Techniques include precision agriculture, agroecology, and integrated pest management, which help in reducing chemical use and preserving biodiversity.

Local and Organic Farming: There is a significant emphasis on local food systems and organic farming, which enhances food security by reducing dependency on imported food and increasing resilience against global market fluctuations.

3. Challenges

Climate Change: Extreme weather events, such as droughts and floods, threaten agricultural productivity. European farmers face increasing pressure to adapt to changing climate conditions.

Food Waste: Approximately one-third of food produced in the EU is wasted. Tackling food waste is essential for improving food security and sustainability.

Market Volatility: Fluctuations in global food prices can impact food affordability and accessibility for vulnerable populations.

4. Social Considerations

Nutrition and Health: European countries focus on ensuring not just food availability but also the nutritional quality of food. Public health campaigns promote healthy eating habits and the consumption of locally produced foods.

Equity and Inclusion: Addressing food insecurity among marginalized communities is a priority. Programs aimed at increasing access to affordable, nutritious food are essential for achieving equitable food security.

Sustainable Food Security in Africa

1. Policy Frameworks and Initiatives

Malabo Declaration: African Union member states committed to enhancing food security, promoting agricultural growth, and eradicating hunger by 2025. This declaration emphasizes investments in agriculture and improving agricultural productivity.

Comprehensive Africa Agriculture Development Programme (CAADP): This initiative aims to increase agricultural productivity and improve food security through evidence-based planning and investment in agriculture.

2. Agricultural Practices

Smallholder Farming: Most food production in Africa comes from smallholder farmers who rely on traditional farming practices. Enhancing their capacity through access to technology, training, and resources is crucial for improving food security.

Climate-Smart Agriculture: Integrating climate-smart practices, such as improved crop varieties, agroforestry, and soil conservation techniques, can enhance resilience to climate change while boosting productivity.

3. Challenges

Poverty and Inequality: High levels of poverty and inequality hinder access to food, particularly for marginalized groups. Addressing socio-economic disparities is critical for achieving food security.

Infrastructure Gaps: Inadequate transportation, storage, and market facilities contribute to food loss and limit farmers' access to markets, affecting food availability and affordability.

Political Instability: Conflicts and governance issues can disrupt food production and distribution, exacerbating food insecurity in affected regions.

4. Social Considerations

Nutritional Challenges: Malnutrition, particularly among children and women, remains a significant concern in Africa. Improving access to diverse, nutritious foods is essential for enhancing food security and public health.

Community Engagement: Involving local communities in decision-making processes regarding food systems can enhance sustainability and ensure that food security initiatives are culturally appropriate and effective.

Comparative Insights

Innovation and Technology: Both Europe and Africa are leveraging technology to improve agricultural productivity. While Europe is advancing precision agriculture and biotech innovations, Africa focuses on mobile technology and community-based solutions to enhance farming practices.

Sustainability Focus: Europe places a strong emphasis on sustainable practices and reducing environmental impacts, while Africa is working to develop its agricultural systems in a way that is economically viable and resilient to climate change.

Food Waste: Europe faces challenges related to food waste at the consumer level, whereas Africa grapples with food loss primarily during production and distribution due to inadequate infrastructure.

Development of Resource (Agricultural) Efficient Bioeconomy

The development of a resource-efficient agricultural bioeconomy focuses on optimizing the use of biological resources to produce food, bio-based products, and energy while minimizing environmental impact. This involves integrating sustainable practices, technology, and innovative management strategies. Below are key components and strategies for developing a resource-efficient agricultural bioeconomy:

1. Sustainable Agricultural Practices

Conservation Agriculture: Emphasizes minimal soil disturbance, cover cropping, and crop rotation to improve soil health, enhance biodiversity, and increase resilience to climate change.

Agroecology: Integrates ecological principles into agricultural systems, promoting biodiversity, natural pest control, and the sustainable use of resources.

Organic Farming: Focuses on using organic inputs and sustainable practices to enhance soil fertility and reduce chemical usage.

2. Technological Innovation

Precision Agriculture: Utilizes technologies like GPS, sensors, and data analytics to monitor crop health, optimize inputs (water, fertilizers, pesticides), and improve yields while reducing waste.

Biotechnology: Involves genetic modifications and innovations like CRISPR to develop crop varieties that are more resilient to pests, diseases, and environmental stresses, increasing productivity and resource efficiency.

Vertical Farming: Allows for year-round production in controlled environments, reducing land use and transportation emissions while optimizing resource inputs such as water and nutrients.

3. Circular Economy Principles

Waste Valorization: Transforming agricultural waste into valuable resources (e.g., bioenergy, fertilizers, and bioplastics) reduces waste and enhances resource efficiency.

Integrated Farming Systems: Combining crops and livestock allows for better nutrient cycling, where waste from one system serves as input for another, minimizing external inputs.

4. Water Management Strategies

Drip Irrigation and Rainwater Harvesting: Efficient water management techniques reduce water usage while ensuring crops receive adequate moisture.

Soil Moisture Management: Techniques like mulching and cover cropping improve soil moisture retention, reducing the need for irrigation.

5. Policy and Governance

Supportive Policies: Governments can promote a resource-efficient bioeconomy through policies that incentivize sustainable practices, provide funding for R&D, and support local food systems.

Regulatory Frameworks: Establishing standards for sustainability and resource use can guide agricultural practices and encourage responsible management of biological resources.

6. Education and Capacity Building

Training Programs: Educating farmers about sustainable practices, new technologies, and resource management enhances their capacity to adopt efficient practices.

Research and Development: Investing in agricultural R&D is essential for developing innovative solutions that improve efficiency and sustainability in the bioeconomy.

7. Market Development

Value Chain Integration: Promoting collaboration among producers, processors, and consumers fosters a more efficient agricultural system that maximizes resource use and reduces waste.

Consumer Awareness: Encouraging consumers to choose sustainably produced food can drive demand for bio-based products and practices.

8. Monitoring and Assessment

Performance Indicators: Establishing metrics to evaluate the sustainability and efficiency of agricultural practices is crucial for continuous improvement and accountability.

Life Cycle Assessment (LCA): This tool helps in assessing the environmental impacts of agricultural products throughout their life cycle, identifying areas for improvement.

Social and Economic Challenges for Bioeconomy

The bioeconomy, which focuses on the sustainable use of biological resources to produce food, energy, and materials, faces various social and economic challenges that can impede its development. Here are some of the key challenges:

1. Economic Disparities

Access to Resources: Smallholder farmers and rural communities often lack access to the financial resources, technology, and infrastructure needed to participate in the bioeconomy.

Investment Gaps: High upfront costs for technology adoption can be a barrier for smaller enterprises, limiting their ability to innovate and compete in bio-based markets.

2. Market Acceptance and Consumer Awareness

Public Perception: There may be skepticism towards genetically modified organisms (GMOs) and bio-based products, which can hinder market acceptance.

Knowledge Gaps: Limited consumer understanding of the benefits and safety of bio-based products can result in lower demand.

3. Regulatory Frameworks

Complex Regulations: Navigating the regulatory landscape for biotechnology can be complicated and time-consuming, discouraging innovation.

Inconsistent Policies: Variations in regulations across regions can create uncertainty for businesses, making it difficult to operate on a larger scale.

4. Social Equity and Inclusion

Marginalization of Communities: The benefits of the bioeconomy may not reach all communities equally, particularly marginalized groups that lack political power or resources.

Job Displacement: Transitioning to a bioeconomy may displace workers in traditional industries, leading to unemployment and social unrest if adequate measures are not taken.

5. Skills and Knowledge Gaps

Workforce Development: There is often a shortage of skilled professionals in biotechnology and bioeconomy sectors, hindering growth and innovation.

Education and Training: Access to education and training programs in bioeconomy-related fields is crucial for developing a competent workforce.

6. Infrastructure Limitations

Inadequate Infrastructure: Insufficient transportation, storage, and processing facilities can limit the efficiency of bio-based supply chains and increase production costs.

Rural Development Needs: Many bioeconomy initiatives are based in rural areas, where infrastructure development is often lacking.

7. Competition with Conventional Industries

Established Markets: Bio-based products often compete with well-established fossil fuel and conventional agricultural industries, which can be resistant to change.

Price Competitiveness: Bio-based alternatives may initially have higher production costs, making it difficult to compete with cheaper conventional products.

8. Environmental and Resource Constraints

Resource Depletion: Unsustainable harvesting of biological resources can lead to depletion, threatening the very basis of the bioeconomy.

Climate Change Impacts: Extreme weather conditions can affect agricultural productivity, making it challenging to ensure a stable supply of biomass.

9. Global Competition

International Market Dynamics: Countries with advanced bioeconomy sectors may dominate global markets, making it difficult for developing nations to compete.

Technology Transfer: Limited access to advanced technologies and innovations can hinder the growth of the bioeconomy in less developed regions.

10. Ethical and Moral Considerations

Biotechnology Ethics: Ethical concerns surrounding genetic engineering and biotechnology can lead to public backlash and regulatory challenges.

Social Acceptance: Cultural attitudes towards biotechnology and bio-based practices can vary widely, influencing acceptance and participation in the bioeconomy.

Forestry Model

The forestry model refers to the strategies and practices used to manage forest resources sustainably while balancing ecological, economic, and social goals. This model aims to ensure that forests can meet current and future needs for timber, non-timber products, and ecosystem services.

Below are key components of a sustainable forestry model:

1. Sustainable Forest Management (SFM)

Definition: SFM is a dynamic process that aims to maintain and enhance the economic, social, and environmental values of forests for present and future generations.

Principles:

Maintain forest biodiversity.

Ensure the long-term health of forest ecosystems.

Balance economic viability with ecological integrity.

Involve stakeholders in decision-making processes.

2. Agroforestry Systems

Integration of Trees and Agriculture: Agroforestry combines trees with crops or livestock, promoting biodiversity and improving soil quality.

Benefits:

Enhances crop yields through improved microclimates and soil health.

Provides additional sources of income (e.g., fruits, nuts, timber).

Contributes to carbon sequestration and biodiversity conservation.

3. Forest Certification

Purpose: Certification programs (e.g., Forest Stewardship Council, FSC) ensure that forests are managed according to sustainable practices.

Benefits: Certified products can command higher prices in the market, providing financial incentives for sustainable management.

4. Community Forestry

Definition: Involves local communities in the management of forest resources, empowering them to make decisions about sustainable practices.

Benefits:

Ensures that local knowledge and needs are incorporated into forest management.

Provides livelihoods and enhances social cohesion within communities.

Increases accountability and reduces deforestation.

5. Ecological Restoration

Restoration Efforts: Focus on rehabilitating degraded forest lands and restoring biodiversity.

Methods: Techniques may include reforestation, afforestation, and the reintroduction of native species.

Benefits: Restored forests can provide ecosystem services, improve water quality, and enhance carbon sequestration.

6. Integrated Pest Management (IPM)

Definition: IPM combines biological, cultural, mechanical, and chemical practices to manage pests sustainably.

Benefits:

Reduces the reliance on chemical pesticides, minimizing environmental impact.

Promotes healthy forest ecosystems by maintaining natural pest control mechanisms.

7. Climate Change Mitigation

Carbon Sequestration: Forests act as carbon sinks, absorbing CO2 from the atmosphere and helping mitigate climate change.

Adaptation Strategies: Implementing practices that enhance the resilience of forests to climate change impacts (e.g., selecting climate-resilient species).

8. Technological Innovations

Remote Sensing and GIS: Technology enables better monitoring of forest health, biomass, and land use changes.

Precision Forestry: Using data analytics and technologies to optimize forest management practices and improve efficiency.

9. Policy and Governance

Regulatory Frameworks: Governments should create policies that support sustainable forestry practices and protect forest ecosystems.

Incentives for Sustainable Practices: Financial incentives, subsidies, and support for sustainable forest management initiatives encourage responsible practices.

10. Economic Viability

Diversification of Forest Products: Beyond timber, forests provide a range of products (e.g., medicinal plants, resins) that can enhance economic returns.

Value-Added Products: Investing in processing facilities can create jobs and increase the economic value of forest products.

Regulation of Renewable Resources

A. Importance of Regulation

Sustainable Use: Regulation ensures that renewable resources (such as forests, fisheries, and water) are used sustainably, preventing over-exploitation and depletion.

Ecosystem Protection: Protects biodiversity and ecosystems, maintaining the health of natural resources.

B. Policy Frameworks

Resource Management Policies: Development of comprehensive policies that govern the sustainable management of renewable resources, such as quotas for fishing, sustainable logging practices, and water use restrictions.

Environmental Regulations: Establishing laws and guidelines that dictate how resources should be used and what practices are acceptable to minimize environmental impact.

C. Certification and Standards

Certification Programs: Encouraging practices like Forest Stewardship Council (FSC) certification, which promotes sustainable forestry practices.

Standards Development: Creating and enforcing standards for the sustainable harvesting of renewable resources, ensuring compliance and accountability.

D. Community Involvement

Stakeholder Engagement: Involving local communities in resource management decisions ensures that regulations are practical and respect traditional knowledge and practices.

Decentralized Management: Empowering local communities to manage resources can lead to better compliance with sustainable practices.

Investing in Agriculture Harvesting Capacity

A. Infrastructure Development

Investment in Facilities: Building and upgrading infrastructure such as storage facilities, transportation networks, and processing plants to reduce post-harvest losses and improve market access.

Irrigation Systems: Investing in efficient irrigation systems to enhance agricultural productivity and resource management.

B. Technological Adoption

Precision Agriculture: Promoting the use of technologies (e.g., GPS, drones, sensors) that optimize input use (water, fertilizers) and increase yields.

Biotechnology: Supporting research and development of genetically modified crops that are resistant to pests and climate variability.

C. Training and Capacity Building

Farmer Education Programs: Providing training for farmers on sustainable agricultural practices, resource management, and technology use to enhance their skills.

Extension Services: Offering agricultural extension services to provide ongoing support and information to farmers.

D. Access to Finance

Microfinancing and Loans: Facilitating access to financial resources for smallholders to invest in equipment and sustainable practices.

Government Grants and Subsidies: Offering financial incentives to encourage investments in sustainable agriculture.

Economic Growth in Bioeconomy

A.Contribution to GDP

Economic Impact: The bioeconomy can significantly contribute to national GDP by generating income from bio-based sectors like agriculture, forestry, and biotechnology.

Job Creation: Expanding bioeconomy sectors leads to new employment opportunities in agriculture, processing, and research.

B. Rural Development

Economic Diversification: Promoting bio-based industries in rural areas provides alternative income sources, reducing reliance on traditional agriculture.

Improved Infrastructure: Investments in bioeconomy initiatives often lead to better infrastructure and services in rural communities.

Development and Innovation in Bioeconomy

A. Research and Development (R&D)

Investment in R&D: Continuous investment in agricultural and biotechnology research fosters innovation, leading to new products and sustainable practices.

Collaboration with Institutions: Partnering with universities, research centers, and industry to drive innovation and technology transfer.

B. Policy Support for Innovation

Incentives for Startups: Creating a favorable environment for startups in the bioeconomy through grants, tax incentives, and access to incubators.

Intellectual Property Protection: Ensuring that innovations are protected through patent systems encourages investment in new technologies.

C. Market Development

Creating Demand for Bio-based Products: Promoting awareness and demand for sustainable bio-based products can drive economic growth and innovation.

Value Chains: Developing efficient value chains that connect producers with consumers, enhancing market access and profitability.

D. Social Innovation

Community-Based Initiatives: Supporting community-led projects that promote sustainable practices and enhance local livelihoods.

Education and Awareness Campaigns: Raising public awareness about the benefits of a bioeconomy, fostering greater acceptance and participation.

Environmental Economics and the Role of Government

A. Definition of Environmental Economics

Focus: Environmental economics studies the economic impact of environmental policies and the economic causes of environmental issues.

Objectives: Aims to understand how economic activities affect the environment and how to design policies that balance economic growth with environmental protection.

B. Government Intervention

Regulatory Frameworks: Governments implement regulations to limit pollution, manage natural resources, and protect ecosystems (e.g., emission standards, resource quotas).

Market-Based Instruments: Utilizing tools like carbon pricing, taxes, and tradable permits to create economic incentives for reducing environmental harm.

Subsidies and Support: Offering financial incentives for sustainable practices, such as renewable energy investments and conservation efforts.

C. Policy Development

Integrated Policy Approaches: Creating cohesive policies that address both economic and environmental goals, considering social equity and sustainability.

Stakeholder Engagement: Involving businesses, communities, and NGOs in policy formulation to ensure that diverse perspectives and needs are addressed.

D. Environmental Valuation

Cost-Benefit Analysis: Evaluating the economic implications of environmental policies to determine their effectiveness and efficiency.

Ecosystem Services Valuation: Recognizing the economic value of ecosystem services (e.g., clean air, water filtration) to inform policy decisions.

Modelling and Tools Supporting the Transition to a Bioeconomy

The transition to a bioeconomy, which focuses on the sustainable use of biological resources for production and services, requires effective modelling and tools to inform decision-making and optimize resource management. Below is a detailed explanation of various models and tools that support this transition.

1. Economic Modelling

A. Types of Economic Models

Input-Output Models: These models analyze the relationships between different sectors of the economy, helping to assess the impacts of changes in bioeconomy sectors on overall economic activity.

Computable General Equilibrium (CGE) Models: CGE models simulate how changes in policies or external factors affect the economy, allowing for the assessment of trade-offs and interactions between different sectors, including bio-based industries.

B. Scenario Analysis

What-If Scenarios: Modelling various policy scenarios (e.g., carbon pricing, subsidies for bioproducts) to evaluate potential economic and environmental outcomes.

Sensitivity Analysis: Evaluating how changes in key assumptions (like resource availability or technological advancements) impact the results of economic models.

2. Decision Support Tools

A. Life Cycle Assessment (LCA)

Definition: LCA evaluates the environmental impacts of a product or process throughout its entire life cycle, from raw material extraction to disposal.

Application: Helps businesses identify opportunities for reducing environmental footprints and improving sustainability in bioproduct development.

B. Environmental Impact Assessment (EIA)

Purpose: EIA assesses the potential environmental impacts of proposed projects or policies before they are implemented.

Importance: Ensures that ecological considerations are integrated into the planning process, promoting sustainable development.

3. Geographic Information Systems (GIS)

A. Spatial Analysis

Mapping Resources: GIS allows for the visualization of geographical data, helping to identify suitable locations for biobased production (e.g., biomass sourcing, bioenergy plants).

Land Use Planning: Supports sustainable land management by analyzing land use patterns and assessing the environmental impact of different agricultural or forestry practices.

B. Decision-Making Support

Site Selection: GIS tools can aid in the site selection for biobased facilities by considering factors such as resource availability, environmental constraints, and logistics.

Biodiversity Conservation: Helps to identify areas that require conservation efforts, supporting the sustainable management of biological resources.

4. Data Collection and Management

A. Big Data Analytics

Data-Driven Insights: Utilizing big data analytics to gather information on resource use, consumer preferences, and environmental impacts to inform decision-making in the bioeconomy.

Predictive Modelling: Applying machine learning algorithms to predict trends in bioeconomy sectors, such as agricultural yields or market demands for bioproducts.

B. Monitoring and Reporting Systems

Tracking Progress: Establishing systems to monitor environmental and economic performance indicators related to the bioeconomy, allowing for adaptive management and policy adjustments.

Transparency and Accountability: Data management systems facilitate transparency in the bioeconomy, enabling stakeholders to assess sustainability claims and compliance with regulations.

5. *Policy Modelling*

A. Policy Impact Assessment

Evaluating Policy Options: Modelling tools help assess the economic and environmental impacts of proposed policies on the bioeconomy, guiding evidence-based decision-making.

Regulatory Framework Development: Informing the design of regulations that promote sustainable practices and encourage investment in bioeconomy sectors.

B. Stakeholder Engagement Tools

Collaborative Modelling: Involving stakeholders in the modelling process to ensure that diverse perspectives are incorporated into decision-making.

Public Participation: Tools that facilitate public engagement and feedback in the planning and implementation of bioeconomy initiatives.

Role of Biobased Economy in Sustainable Development

A.Definition of Biobased Economy

Overview: The biobased economy is an economic system that utilizes renewable biological resources (such as crops, forestry, and waste) for the production of food, materials, and energy.

Goals: Aims to reduce dependency on fossil fuels, minimize environmental impact, and promote sustainable practices.

B. Contributions to Sustainable Development

Resource Efficiency: Enhancing resource use efficiency through sustainable practices, reducing waste, and promoting circular economy principles.

Climate Change Mitigation: Utilizing biobased resources can lead to lower greenhouse gas emissions compared to fossil fuels, contributing to climate change mitigation.

C. Economic Opportunities

Job Creation: The biobased economy can generate employment in agriculture, processing, and research, particularly in rural areas.

Innovation and Growth: Promoting research and development in biobased technologies fosters innovation, driving economic growth and competitiveness.

D. Social Equity and Inclusion

Rural Development: Supporting rural communities by providing new economic opportunities and enhancing local livelihoods through sustainable practices.

Food Security: Ensuring a stable supply of food and renewable resources, contributing to food security and resilience against market fluctuations.

E. Policy and Governance

Supportive Regulatory Frameworks: Developing policies that promote the growth of the biobased economy, such as subsidies for bioproducts and sustainable agricultural practices.

Public-Private Partnerships: Encouraging collaboration between governments, businesses, and communities to foster innovation and investment in the biobased sector.

III

BIOECONOMY RESEARCH

Inter- and Transdisciplinarity in Bioeconomy & Research Approaches

The bioeconomy encompasses various disciplines, integrating knowledge from biology, economics, technology, and social sciences to develop sustainable practices around biobased resources.

1. Interdisciplinarity

Definition: Interdisciplinarity involves the collaboration of different academic disciplines to address complex problems. In the bioeconomy, this means integrating insights from biology, environmental science, economics, and policy studies.

Importance: By combining diverse fields, researchers can develop holistic solutions to challenges like resource scarcity, environmental degradation, and climate change.

2. Transdisciplinarity

Definition: Transdisciplinarity extends beyond academia, involving stakeholders such as industry, government, and local communities in research processes.

Importance: Engaging with non-academic stakeholders ensures that research is relevant and addresses real-world issues, enhancing the applicability of findings in practical contexts.

3. Research Approaches

Systems Thinking: Emphasizing the interconnectedness of ecological, economic, and social systems, systems thinking allows researchers to understand the broader implications of bioeconomy strategies.

Participatory Research: Involving communities and stakeholders in the research process fosters local knowledge and enhances the relevance of findings.

Applied Research: Focused on practical applications, applied research aims to develop technologies and practices that can be implemented in the bioeconomy.

Primary Production and Processing of Biobased Resources

The primary production and processing of biobased resources are fundamental components of the bioeconomy, enabling the sustainable use of biological materials for food, energy, and industrial products. This detailed explanation explores the processes involved, challenges, and innovations associated with these stages.

1. Primary Production of Biobased Resources

A. Definition and Importance

Primary Production: Refers to the initial stage of the bioeconomy where biological resources, such as crops, livestock, and forestry products, are cultivated and harvested.

Importance: Primary production provides the raw materials necessary for various industries, including food, pharmaceuticals, bioenergy, and bioplastics.

B. Types of Biobased Resources

Agricultural Crops: Includes food crops (e.g., grains, fruits, vegetables) and industrial crops (e.g., sugarcane, oilseeds, fibers).

Forestry Products: Timber, non-timber forest products (e.g., resins, medicinal plants), and biomass for energy.

Aquaculture: The farming of fish, shellfish, and aquatic plants, contributing to food security and economic development.

C. Sustainable Practices

Agroecology: Implementing ecological principles in agricultural practices to enhance biodiversity, soil health, and resilience.

Precision Agriculture: Utilizing technology (e.g., GPS, sensors) to optimize resource use (water, fertilizers) and improve crop yields.

Integrated Pest Management (IPM): Combining biological, cultural, and chemical practices to manage pests sustainably, reducing reliance on synthetic pesticides.

D. Challenges in Primary Production

Resource Scarcity: Limited availability of land, water, and nutrients poses challenges to increasing production.

Climate Change: Changing weather patterns, extreme events, and shifting growing seasons affect crop yields and livestock productivity.

Market Access: Farmers may face difficulties accessing markets and securing fair prices for their products, particularly in developing regions.

2. *Processing of Biobased Resources*

A. Definition and Importance

Processing: The transformation of raw biobased materials into value-added products through various physical, chemical, or biological methods.

Importance: Processing enhances the value of biobased resources, creating products that are essential for human consumption, energy production, and industrial applications.

B. Types of Processing Methods

Mechanical Processing: Involves physical methods, such as grinding, milling, and pressing, to convert raw materials into usable forms (e.g., flour from grains).

Thermochemical Processing: Includes processes like pyrolysis and gasification, which convert biomass into biofuels and chemicals through high-temperature reactions.

Biochemical Processing: Utilizes biological processes, such as fermentation, to convert sugars and starches into bioethanol, biogas, and other bioproducts.

C. Key Technologies in Processing

Enzymatic Processing: The use of enzymes to break down complex carbohydrates into simple sugars, facilitating fermentation processes and improving efficiency.

Sustainable Chemical Processes: Developing green chemistry approaches to minimize waste and energy consumption in the production of biobased chemicals.

Advanced Bioreactors: Utilizing bioreactors to optimize fermentation conditions for the production of bioproducts, enhancing yields and reducing processing time.

D. Value Addition and Product Development

Food Products: Transforming agricultural commodities into processed foods, beverages, and nutraceuticals, enhancing nutritional value and safety.

Biofuels: Converting biomass into renewable fuels (e.g., biodiesel, bioethanol) that can replace fossil fuels, contributing to energy security.

Bioplastics and Materials: Developing biobased plastics and materials that are biodegradable or recyclable, reducing environmental impact.

3. Sustainability Considerations

A. Environmental Impact

Resource Management: Implementing practices that ensure sustainable resource use, minimize waste, and reduce emissions associated with production and processing.

Circular Economy: Emphasizing waste reduction and the recycling of biobased materials to create closed-loop systems that enhance sustainability.

B. Social and Economic Aspects

Community Engagement: Involving local communities in decision-making processes related to biobased production and processing to ensure equitable benefits.

Fair Trade Practices: Promoting fair pricing and ethical practices in the supply chain to support farmers and workers involved in primary production.

C. Policy Support

Regulatory Frameworks: Establishing policies that encourage sustainable agricultural practices, support innovation in processing technologies, and promote market access for biobased products.

Research and Development: Investing in R&D to develop new technologies and practices that improve the efficiency and sustainability of biobased production and processing.

Markets, Sustainability Management, and Entrepreneurship in Biobased Products

The integration of biobased products into the market presents unique opportunities and challenges. This section explores the dynamics of markets for biobased products, sustainability management practices, and the role of entrepreneurship in fostering innovation and growth in the bioeconomy.

1. Markets for Biobased Products

A. Definition and Scope

Biobased Products: These are materials and products derived from renewable biological resources, including food, feed, biofuels, biochemicals, and bioplastics.

Market Dynamics: The demand for biobased products is influenced by factors such as consumer preferences, environmental regulations, and advancements in technology.

B. Market Segments

Food and Beverages: Includes organic foods, functional foods, and plant-based alternatives, driven by health consciousness and sustainability trends.

Biofuels: Renewable energy sources derived from biomass, such as biodiesel and bioethanol, used as substitutes for fossil fuels.

Bioplastics and Packaging: Biodegradable plastics and sustainable packaging solutions gaining traction due to environmental concerns over plastic waste.

C. Trends Influencing Markets

Consumer Awareness: Growing awareness of sustainability issues leads consumers to prefer eco-friendly products, driving demand for biobased alternatives.

Regulatory Support: Government policies promoting renewable resources and sustainable practices can create favorable market conditions for biobased products.

Corporate Commitments: Companies increasingly commit to sustainability goals, integrating biobased products into their supply chains to meet consumer demands and regulatory requirements.

D. Market Challenges

Cost Competitiveness: Biobased products may face higher production costs compared to conventional products, necessitating cost-reduction strategies.

Infrastructure Limitations: Limited infrastructure for the production and distribution of biobased products can hinder market development.

Consumer Acceptance: Educating consumers about the benefits and quality of biobased products is essential to enhance market penetration.

2. Sustainability Management in Biobased Products

A. Definition and Importance

Sustainability Management: Involves strategies and practices aimed at minimizing environmental impact, ensuring social equity, and achieving economic viability in the production and consumption of biobased products.

Importance: Sustainable management practices are essential for the long-term success of biobased industries and for addressing global challenges such as climate change and resource depletion.

B. Key Components of Sustainability Management

Life Cycle Assessment (LCA): Evaluates the environmental impacts of biobased products throughout their life cycle, from raw material extraction to disposal. LCA helps identify opportunities for improvement and informs decision-making.

Sustainable Sourcing: Ensuring that raw materials are sourced from environmentally responsible and socially equitable suppliers, promoting sustainable agriculture and forestry practices.

Waste Management: Implementing strategies to reduce waste generation and promote recycling and reuse of materials in biobased product supply chains.

C. Certification and Standards

Sustainability Certifications: Various certifications (e.g., USDA Organic, Forest Stewardship Council) help consumers identify sustainable products, promoting market confidence.

Regulatory Compliance: Adhering to environmental regulations and standards ensures that biobased products meet safety and sustainability criteria.

D. Challenges in Sustainability Management

Balancing Trade-offs: Achieving a balance between economic viability and environmental sustainability can be challenging, especially for small-scale producers.

Data Availability: Limited access to reliable data on environmental impacts and supply chain practices can hinder effective sustainability management.

3. Entrepreneurship in Biobased Products

A. Role of Entrepreneurship

Innovation and Growth: Entrepreneurs drive innovation in the biobased sector by developing new products, processes, and business models that enhance sustainability and efficiency.

Job Creation: The growth of biobased industries leads to job creation in production, processing, and distribution, contributing to economic development.

B. Opportunities for Entrepreneurs

Market Niches: Entrepreneurs can target emerging markets for biobased products, such as plant-based foods, biodegradable packaging, and renewable energy solutions.

Collaboration: Partnering with research institutions, government agencies, and other businesses can foster innovation and access to resources.

Access to Funding: Various funding sources, including government grants, venture capital, and impact investment, support entrepreneurial ventures in the biobased sector.

C. Challenges for Entrepreneurs

Market Competition: Entrepreneurs may face competition from established industries and conventional products, necessitating differentiation strategies.

Regulatory Hurdles: Navigating complex regulations and obtaining necessary certifications can be time-consuming and costly for startups.

Scaling Production: Transitioning from small-scale production to commercial-scale operations presents logistical and financial challenges.

D. Support for Entrepreneurial Endeavors

Incubators and Accelerators: Programs that provide mentorship, resources, and networking opportunities for startups in the biobased sector.

Education and Training: Providing training programs that equip entrepreneurs with the knowledge and skills needed to succeed in the bioeconomy.

Biobased Resources and Value Chains

The concept of biobased resources and value chains is central to the bioeconomy, emphasizing the sustainable use of biological materials to create value-added products. This section details the types of biobased resources, their processing, and how value chains are structured to optimize resource utilization and economic benefits.

1. Biobased Resources

A. Definition and Types

Biobased Resources: Materials derived from living organisms, including plants, animals, and microorganisms, that can be used for food, feed, energy, and industrial products.

Types of Biobased Resources:

Agricultural Biomass: Crops (e.g., grains, oilseeds, fruits) and residues (e.g., straw, husks) that can be used for food, biofuels, or biochemicals.

Forestry Biomass: Timber, wood residues, and non-timber forest products (e.g., resins, medicinal plants) that contribute to various industries.

Aquatic Biomass: Includes fish, shellfish, and seaweeds that provide food, feed, and raw materials for bioproducts.

Microbial Biomass: Microorganisms used in fermentation processes to produce biofuels, enzymes, and other bioproducts.

B. Importance of Biobased Resources

Renewability: Biobased resources are renewable, providing an alternative to fossil fuels and synthetic materials.

Carbon Sequestration: The cultivation of biobased resources can capture carbon dioxide, contributing to climate change mitigation.

Economic Opportunities: The utilization of biobased resources can create jobs and promote rural development through diversified agricultural practices.

2. Processing of Biobased Resources

A. Overview of Processing

Definition: Processing involves converting raw biobased materials into usable products through various physical, chemical, or biological methods.

Goals: The primary goals of processing are to enhance the value of raw materials, improve product quality, and ensure sustainability.

B. Key Processing Methods

Mechanical Processing: Physical methods such as grinding, milling, and pressing to prepare raw materials (e.g., flour from grains, oils from seeds).

Thermochemical Processing: High-temperature methods (e.g., pyrolysis, gasification) that convert biomass into biofuels and chemicals through chemical reactions.

Biochemical Processing: Utilizes microorganisms or enzymes to transform organic matter into products such as bioethanol, biogas, and other biochemicals.

C. Innovations in Processing

Enzymatic Processing: Using specific enzymes to improve efficiency in breaking down complex carbohydrates, enhancing fermentation processes, and increasing yields.

Integrated Biorefineries: Facilities that process multiple biobased feedstocks to produce a range of products (e.g., fuels, chemicals, food) from a single biomass source, maximizing resource utilization.

Sustainable Practices: Implementing circular economy principles, where waste from one process serves as a resource for another, minimizing environmental impact.

3. Value Chains for Biobased Products

A. Definition of Value Chains

Value Chain: The full range of activities involved in bringing a biobased product from conception to market, including production, processing, distribution, and consumption.

Importance: A well-structured value chain enhances efficiency, reduces costs, and improves competitiveness in the biobased sector.

B. Key Components of Value Chains

Input Supply: Providers of seeds, fertilizers, and equipment necessary for agricultural production.

Production: Farmers and producers who cultivate crops or raise livestock, focusing on sustainable practices to optimize yield and quality.

Processing: Facilities that transform raw materials into final products, using various processing techniques to add value.

Distribution: Logistics and supply chain management that ensure products reach consumers efficiently, including warehousing, transportation, and retailing.

Consumption: End-users, including consumers and industries, that drive demand for biobased products based on sustainability and quality considerations.

C. Optimization of Value Chains

Collaboration: Encouraging collaboration among stakeholders (farmers, processors, distributors) to share resources, knowledge, and best practices.

Market Research: Understanding consumer preferences and trends to align production and processing with market demands.

Technology Integration: Utilizing digital technologies (e.g., blockchain, IoT) to enhance traceability, transparency, and efficiency throughout the value chain.

D. Challenges in Value Chains

Fragmentation: Many biobased value chains are fragmented, with small producers struggling to compete in larger markets.

Access to Markets: Limited access to markets for small-scale producers can hinder their participation in the value chain.

Regulatory Hurdles: Navigating complex regulations can pose challenges for businesses involved in biobased product development and marketing.

Processing of Biobased Resources

A. Overview of Processing

Definition: The processing of biobased resources involves converting raw biological materials into usable products through various methods, including physical, chemical, and biological techniques.

Objectives: The main objectives include enhancing product quality, increasing yield, and ensuring the sustainability of the production process.

B. Key Processing Techniques

Mechanical Processing: Involves physical alterations, such as grinding, crushing, or pressing, to prepare raw materials. For example, milling grains into flour or pressing oil from seeds.

Thermochemical Processing: Utilizes heat and chemical reactions to convert biomass into biofuels (like bioethanol) and other chemicals.

Processes include pyrolysis, gasification, and combustion.

Biochemical Processing: Relies on biological agents (enzymes and microorganisms) to convert organic matter into valuable products. Fermentation is a common method for producing alcohols and organic acids.

C. Innovations in Processing

Integrated Biorefineries: Facilities that convert biomass into a range of products, including fuels, chemicals, and materials, optimizing resource utilization and minimizing waste.

Green Chemistry: Implementing environmentally friendly chemical processes that reduce the use of hazardous substances and energy consumption.

Circular Economy Practices: Establishing processes that utilize waste products from one stage as inputs for another, enhancing sustainability.

Markets for Biobased Products

A. Market Dynamics

Definition: The market for biobased products encompasses the demand and supply of products derived from biological materials.

Growth Factors: Increasing consumer awareness of sustainability, government policies promoting renewable resources, and technological advancements drive the growth of biobased markets.

B. Key Market Segments

Food and Beverages: Includes organic and plant-based foods, which are increasingly popular among health-conscious consumers.

Biofuels: Renewable energy sources like biodiesel and bioethanol, crucial for reducing dependence on fossil fuels.

Bioplastics and Packaging: Biodegradable alternatives to traditional plastics, gaining traction due to environmental concerns.

C. Challenges in Market Development

Cost Competitiveness: Biobased products often have higher production costs, making them less competitive compared to conventional products.

Infrastructure Needs: Limited infrastructure for the production, distribution, and recycling of biobased products can hinder market growth.

Consumer Acceptance: Educating consumers about the benefits and quality of biobased products is essential for enhancing market penetration.

Sustainability Management in Biobased Products

A. Importance of Sustainability Management

Definition: Sustainability management involves strategies to minimize environmental impact while maximizing social and economic benefits in the production and use of biobased products.

Goals: The main goals include reducing greenhouse gas emissions, ensuring resource efficiency, and promoting social equity.

B. Key Components of Sustainability Management

Life Cycle Assessment (LCA): A method for evaluating the environmental impacts associated with all stages of a product's life, from raw material extraction to disposal.

Sustainable Sourcing: Prioritizing the use of renewable resources that are produced responsibly and ethically, ensuring that supply chains are sustainable.

Waste Management: Implementing practices to minimize waste generation and promote recycling, composting, and repurposing of biobased materials.

C. Regulatory and Certification Frameworks

Sustainability Certifications: Certifications such as USDA Organic or Fair Trade help consumers identify sustainable products and build market confidence.

Compliance: Adhering to environmental regulations ensures that biobased products meet safety and sustainability standards.

Entrepreneurship Opportunities in Biobased Products

A. Role of Entrepreneurship

Innovation Driver: Entrepreneurs play a crucial role in developing new products and processes that enhance sustainability and efficiency in the biobased sector.

Economic Impact: Biobased entrepreneurship contributes to job creation and economic growth, particularly in rural and agricultural communities.

B. Opportunities for Entrepreneurs

Niche Markets: Identifying and targeting emerging markets for biobased products, such as plant-based foods, biodegradable packaging, and natural chemicals.

Collaboration and Partnerships: Forming partnerships with research institutions, government agencies, and other businesses to share resources and foster innovation.

Access to Funding: Entrepreneurs can tap into various funding sources, including government grants, venture capital, and impact investments aimed at sustainable ventures.

C. Challenges for Entrepreneurs

Market Competition: Competing with established industries and traditional products can be challenging for new entrants.

Regulatory Hurdles: Navigating complex regulations and obtaining necessary certifications can be time-consuming and costly.

Scaling Production: Transitioning from small-scale production to commercial-scale operations presents logistical and financial challenges.

D. Support for Biobased Entrepreneurship

Incubators and Accelerators: Programs that provide mentorship, funding, and resources for startups in the biobased sector.

Education and Training: Offering educational programs to equip entrepreneurs with the necessary skills and knowledge to succeed in the bioeconomy.

Food Security and Healthy Nutrition in the Context of the Bioeconomy

Food security and healthy nutrition are critical components of global development, closely intertwined with the bioeconomy. The bioeconomy offers innovative approaches to enhance food production, improve nutrition, and ensure sustainable practices. This section explores the relationship between food security, nutrition, and the bioeconomy.

1. Understanding Food Security

A. Definition of Food Security

Food Security: The condition in which all people, at all times, have physical, social, and economic access to sufficient, safe, and nutritious food to meet their dietary needs for an active and healthy life.

Components of Food Security:

Availability: Sufficient quantities of food produced or imported.

Access: Economic and physical access to food.

Utilization: Nutritional quality and safety of food consumed.

Stability: Consistent access to food over time.

B. Global Food Security Challenges

Population Growth: The rising global population increases demand for food, necessitating higher agricultural productivity.

Climate Change: Environmental changes threaten crop yields and food supply chains, exacerbating food insecurity.

Economic Inequality: Disparities in wealth and resources lead to unequal access to food, impacting marginalized communities.

2. *Healthy Nutrition*

A. Importance of Healthy Nutrition

Definition: Healthy nutrition refers to a balanced diet that provides essential nutrients to maintain health, prevent diseases, and promote well-being.

Key Nutrients: Proteins, carbohydrates, fats, vitamins, and minerals are crucial for physical health, cognitive development, and overall quality of life.

B. Impact of Nutrition on Health

Chronic Diseases: Poor nutrition is linked to obesity, diabetes, heart disease, and other chronic conditions.

Child Development: Adequate nutrition is vital for growth and development in children, influencing cognitive and physical abilities.

3. *The Role of the Bioeconomy in Food Security and Nutrition*

A. Sustainable Agricultural Practices

Biobased Innovations: Utilizing biobased resources and innovative agricultural practices, such as agroecology, precision farming, and organic farming, enhances food production while minimizing environmental impact.

Crop Diversification: Promoting diverse crops improves resilience against pests and diseases, ensuring stable food supplies and reducing dependency on a few staple crops.

B. Nutritional Enhancement of Food Products

Biofortification: The process of increasing the nutritional value of crops through conventional breeding or biotechnology (e.g., Golden Rice enriched with vitamin A) to combat malnutrition.

Functional Foods: Development of foods that provide health benefits beyond basic nutrition, such as probiotics, omega-3 enriched products, and fortified foods.

C. Waste Reduction and Resource Efficiency

Value Chain Optimization: Implementing circular economy principles in the food supply chain to minimize waste, enhance resource use efficiency, and ensure that surplus food is redirected to those in need.

Bioconversion: Transforming food waste into valuable products (e.g., animal feed, bioenergy) to reduce environmental impact and enhance food security.

4. *Policy and Governance in the Bioeconomy*

A. Supportive Policies for Food Security

Government Initiatives: Policies that promote sustainable agricultural practices, support local farmers, and ensure access to nutritious food can enhance food security.

International Cooperation: Collaborative efforts among countries to address global food security challenges and share best practices in sustainable agriculture and nutrition.

B. Stakeholder Engagement

Community Involvement: Engaging local communities in decision-making processes related to food production and nutrition can lead to more effective solutions tailored to local needs.

Public-Private Partnerships: Collaborations between governments, private sector players, and non-profit organizations can drive innovations in food production and distribution.

5. *Challenges and Future Directions*

A. Addressing Barriers to Food Security

Infrastructure Development: Improving transportation and storage facilities to reduce food loss and ensure access to markets.

Research and Development: Investing in R&D to develop new technologies and practices that enhance agricultural productivity and nutritional quality.

B. Promoting Awareness and Education

Nutrition Education: Raising awareness about the importance of healthy eating and providing education on food preparation and nutrition can empower individuals to make informed choices.

Sustainable Practices Education: Training farmers and communities in sustainable agricultural practices to improve resilience and productivity.

Use of Biomass for the Production of Fuel and Chemicals

Biomass refers to organic materials derived from plants, animals, and microorganisms that can be utilized for energy and chemical production. The use of biomass is a crucial aspect of the bioeconomy, as it offers renewable alternatives to fossil fuels and synthetic chemicals, contributing to sustainability and reducing greenhouse gas emissions.

1. Biomass Feedstocks

A. Types of Biomass Feedstocks

Lignocellulosic Biomass: Composed of cellulose, hemicellulose, and lignin, found in agricultural residues (e.g., straw, corn stover), forestry residues, and dedicated energy crops (e.g., switchgrass, miscanthus).

Algal Biomass: Microalgae and macroalgae are rich in lipids, carbohydrates, and proteins, making them suitable for biofuels and biochemicals.

Waste Biomass: Includes organic waste from agriculture (e.g., food waste), forestry (e.g., sawdust), and municipal sources that can be converted into fuels or chemicals.

2. Biomass Conversion Technologies

A. Thermochemical Processes

Combustion: Direct burning of biomass to generate heat and power.

Gasification: Converting biomass into syngas (a mixture of hydrogen and carbon monoxide) through high-temperature reactions, which can be further processed into fuels or chemicals.

Pyrolysis: Decomposing biomass at high temperatures in the absence of oxygen to produce bio-oil, biochar, and syngas.

B. Biochemical Processes

Fermentation: Utilizing microorganisms to convert sugars from biomass into biofuels (e.g., bioethanol, butanol) and other chemicals.

Anaerobic Digestion: Breaking down organic matter by microorganisms in the absence of oxygen to produce biogas (methane) and digestate, which can be used as fertilizer.

C. Chemical Processes

Transesterification: Converting fats and oils from biomass into biodiesel through a chemical reaction with alcohol.

Hydrolysis: Breaking down complex carbohydrates into simple sugars for fermentation or further chemical processing.

3. Applications of Biomass-derived Fuels and Chemicals

A. Biofuels

Bioethanol: Commonly produced from sugarcane, corn, or other starchy materials, used as a gasoline substitute or additive.

Biodiesel: Derived from vegetable oils or animal fats, used in diesel engines as a renewable fuel.

Biogas: Produced through anaerobic digestion, utilized for heating, electricity generation, or as a vehicle fuel.

B. Biochemicals

Bioplastics: Biobased plastics derived from biomass, offering biodegradable alternatives to conventional plastics.

Organic Acids: Such as lactic acid and succinic acid, produced through fermentation for use in food, pharmaceuticals, and biodegradable polymers.

Solvents and Additives: Chemicals derived from biomass for use in various industrial applications, including solvents for paints and coatings.

The Importance of Biotechnology for the Bioeconomy

Biotechnology plays a pivotal role in advancing the bioeconomy by enabling the efficient utilization of biological resources. Through innovative techniques, biotechnology enhances productivity, sustainability, and the development of biobased products.

1. Key Biotechnological Approaches

A. Genetic Engineering

Crop Improvement: Genetically modifying crops to enhance yield, resistance to pests and diseases, and nutritional quality (e.g., biofortified crops).

Microbial Engineering: Modifying microorganisms to improve their efficiency in producing biofuels and biochemicals through fermentation processes.

B. Synthetic Biology

Designing Microbial Factories: Engineering microbes to produce specific products (e.g., pharmaceuticals, biofuels) more efficiently and sustainably.

Metabolic Pathway Engineering: Optimizing metabolic pathways in microorganisms for increased production of desired compounds from biomass.

2. *Applications of Biotechnology in the Bioeconomy*

A. Agricultural Biotechnology

Sustainable Farming Practices: Biopesticides and biofertilizers developed through biotechnology promote sustainable agriculture and reduce reliance on chemical inputs.

Precision Agriculture: Utilizing biotechnological tools for soil health monitoring, crop health assessments, and optimizing resource use.

B. Industrial Biotechnology

Bioprocessing: Using enzymes and microorganisms for more efficient production processes in various industries, such as food and beverages, textiles, and pharmaceuticals.

Waste Valorization: Converting agricultural and industrial waste into valuable products through biotechnological methods.

3. *Environmental and Economic Benefits*

A. Environmental Impact

Reduction of Greenhouse Gas Emissions: Biomass use and biotechnological innovations can significantly lower emissions compared to fossil fuel consumption.

Resource Efficiency: Biotechnology enables the more efficient use of water, land, and nutrients in agricultural production, promoting sustainability.

B. Economic Growth

Job Creation: The growth of the biobased sector fosters job opportunities in agriculture, processing, and biotechnology research.

Rural Development: Promoting biobased industries in rural areas can lead to economic diversification and improved livelihoods for farmers.

IV

ENTREPRENEURSHIP OPPORTUNITY IN AGRI BIOTECHNOLOGY

Business Opportunity

A. Plant Cell and Tissue Culture Techniques

Description: This technique involves growing plant cells in controlled conditions to produce clones or large quantities of specific plants.

Opportunity: High demand for disease-free, high-yielding plants in agriculture and horticulture.

B. Polyhouse Culture

Description: A controlled environment system that allows for the cultivation of plants with optimized conditions (temperature, humidity, and light).

Opportunity: Increased production of high-value crops like flowers and vegetables, especially in regions with adverse climatic conditions.

C. Herbal Bulk Drug Production

Description: The process of cultivating medicinal plants for extracting active pharmaceutical ingredients.

Opportunity: Growing global demand for herbal medicine due to a shift towards natural products.

D. Nutraceuticals and Value-Added Herbal Products

Description: Nutraceuticals are food products with health benefits, while value-added herbal products include enhanced herbal extracts.

Opportunity: Rising consumer awareness of health and wellness fuels demand for these products.

E. Bioethanol Production Using Agricultural Waste

Description: Converting agricultural residues (e.g., corn stover, sugarcane bagasse) into bioethanol.

Opportunity: Growing interest in renewable energy and reducing reliance on fossil fuels.

F. Algal Sources for Biofuels

Description: Utilizing algae to produce biofuels and other high-value products.

Opportunity: Algae can grow rapidly and can be cultivated on non-arable land, presenting a sustainable energy source.

G. Integration of System Biology for Agricultural Applications

Description: Applying systems biology approaches to optimize crop traits and management.

Opportunity: Enhances crop resilience and productivity, addressing food security challenges.

H. Biosensor Development in Agri Management

Description: Creating biosensors for monitoring soil health, crop health, and pest detection.

Opportunity: Precision agriculture tools improve resource use efficiency and yield.

Essential Requirements

Research and Development: Significant investment in R&D to develop efficient techniques and products.

Skilled Workforce: Trained personnel in biotechnology, horticulture, and agronomy.

Infrastructure: Adequate laboratory facilities, greenhouses, and processing units.

Regulatory Compliance: Adherence to agricultural and environmental regulations.

Marketing Strategies

A. Plant Cell and Tissue Culture

Target Market: Nurseries, agricultural cooperatives, and large-scale farmers.

Marketing Strategies: Demonstrations, workshops, and partnerships with agricultural extension services.

B. Polyhouse Culture

Target Market: Commercial farmers, horticulturists, and agri-entrepreneurs.

Marketing Strategies: Showcasing success stories, providing consultation services, and offering financing options.

C. Herbal Bulk Drug Production

Target Market: Pharmaceutical companies and health product manufacturers.

Marketing Strategies: Highlighting quality and efficacy, attending trade fairs, and building strong relationships with manufacturers.

D. Nutraceuticals and Value-Added Products

Target Market: Health-conscious consumers, retailers, and online platforms.

Marketing Strategies: Branding as organic/natural, leveraging social media, and influencer partnerships.

E. Bioethanol Production

Target Market: Energy companies and transportation sector.

Marketing Strategies: Emphasizing environmental benefits and cost-effectiveness.

F. Algal Biofuels

Target Market: Biofuel producers and environmentally-conscious companies.

Marketing Strategies: Research collaborations and partnerships for product development.

G. System Biology Applications

Target Market: Agricultural companies and research institutions.

Marketing Strategies: Collaborating with universities and agricultural tech firms for pilot projects.

H. Biosensor Development

Target Market: Farmers, agronomists, and agricultural technology companies.

Marketing Strategies: Demonstrating effectiveness in increasing yield and reducing resource inputs.

Government Schemes and Support

Subsidies and Grants: Financial support for R&D, infrastructure development, and technology adoption.

Tax Incentives: Benefits for investments in sustainable agricultural practices.

Training Programs: Government-sponsored programs for skill development in biotechnology and agriculture.

Partnerships with Universities: Collaborations for research and innovation in agricultural biotechnology.

Challenges

Technological Limitations: High costs and complexities associated with developing and scaling biotechnological processes.

Market Competition: Competing with established agricultural and pharmaceutical sectors.

Regulatory Hurdles: Navigating complex regulations related to biotechnology and health products.

Consumer Acceptance: Overcoming skepticism regarding genetically modified and biotechnological products.

Resource Availability: Ensuring a sustainable supply of raw materials for biomass production.

Scope for Future Development

Sustainable Practices: Increasing focus on sustainability will drive demand for biobased products.

Global Health Trends: The rise in chronic diseases and health awareness will expand the market for nutraceuticals and herbal products.

Technological Advancements: Innovations in biotechnology and precision agriculture will enhance productivity and efficiency.

Policy Support: Governments are likely to continue supporting the bioeconomy, opening new avenues for investment and growth.

Case Study: Biobased Innovations in Agriculture and Biotechnology

1. Plant Cell and Tissue Culture Technique

Background:
Plant cell and tissue culture is a biotechnological technique used to grow plant cells in a controlled environment, enabling the mass propagation of genetically identical plants.

Implementation:

Company: GreenGen Technologies, an Indian startup focusing on producing disease-free high-yield crops.

Process: GreenGen uses tissue culture to propagate high-value crops such as orchids and medicinal plants. The process includes:

Selection of Explants: Choosing healthy plant parts (e.g., stem, leaf) for culture.

Sterilization: Using sterilizing agents to prevent contamination.

Culture Media Preparation: Utilizing nutrient-rich media (MS medium) for plant cell growth.

Subculturing: Regularly transferring cells to fresh media to ensure healthy growth.

Outcome:

Increased Production: Achieved a production rate of 1 million plants annually.

Market Demand: Supplied plants to nurseries, contributing to increased biodiversity and availability of ornamental plants.

2. Polyhouse Culture

Background:
Polyhouse culture refers to the cultivation of plants under controlled environmental conditions using a greenhouse structure.

Implementation:

Farm: EcoFresh Farms, located in a semi-arid region of India.

Structure: EcoFresh established multiple polyhouses equipped with climate control systems (heating, cooling, and ventilation).

Crops Grown: Focused on high-value crops such as tomatoes, cucumbers, and bell peppers.

Techniques Used:

Drip Irrigation: Efficient water use through a drip system.

Nutrient Film Technique (NFT): Ensured optimal nutrient delivery to plants.

Outcome:

Increased Yields: Crop yield increased by 30% compared to open-field cultivation.

Market Position: Positioned as a leading supplier of fresh vegetables to urban markets.

3. Herbal Bulk Drug Production

Background:
The growing demand for herbal medicine has opened opportunities for the production of bulk herbal drugs.

Implementation:

Company: Herbal Pharma Ltd., focused on the production of standardized herbal extracts.

Cultivation: Established organic farms for key medicinal plants such as Ashwagandha and Tulsi.

Extraction Process: Utilized advanced extraction methods (e.g., supercritical CO2 extraction) to obtain high-quality extracts.

Quality Control: Implemented strict quality assurance measures to ensure the efficacy of herbal products.

Outcome:

Market Expansion: Successfully partnered with pharmaceutical companies for supply agreements.

Sustainability: Adopted sustainable farming practices, promoting biodiversity and environmental health.

4. Nutraceuticals and Value-Added Herbal Products

Background:
Nutraceuticals are food products that offer health benefits beyond basic nutrition, including functional foods and dietary supplements.

Implementation:

Company: NutraLife Corp., focusing on developing nutraceuticals from herbal sources.

Product Development: Developed products like herbal teas, fortified snacks, and dietary supplements.

Research and Development: Invested in R&D to explore the health benefits of various herbs and their applications in nutraceuticals.

Outcome:

Sales Growth: Achieved a 50% increase in sales within two years due to rising health consciousness among consumers.

Market Recognition: Awarded for innovation in developing value-added herbal products.

5. *Bioethanol Production Using Agricultural Waste*

Background:
Bioethanol production from agricultural waste provides a sustainable alternative to fossil fuels.

Implementation:

Project: AgriBio Fuels, an initiative to convert agricultural residues (e.g., rice straw, sugarcane bagasse) into bioethanol.

Process:

Pretreatment: Agricultural waste is treated to break down lignin and hemicellulose.

Fermentation: Yeast is used to ferment the sugars released during pretreatment into ethanol.

Distillation: Ethanol is purified through distillation.

Outcome:

Production Capacity: The facility achieved a production capacity of 10,000 liters of bioethanol per day.

Environmental Impact: Reduced waste disposal problems while contributing to renewable energy production.

6. *Algal Sources for Biofuel Production*

Background:
Algae are an attractive source of biofuels due to their rapid growth rates and high lipid content.

Implementation:

Company: AlgaBio Energy, focused on algae cultivation for biofuel production.

Cultivation Method: Implemented open pond systems and photobioreactors to grow microalgae.

Extraction Process: Utilized mechanical and chemical methods to extract oils from algae, which are then converted to biodiesel.

Outcome:

Sustainability: AlgaBio Energy produced biodiesel with a significantly lower carbon footprint than traditional fossil fuels.

Market Demand: Positioned as a leader in the algae biofuel market, securing contracts with biofuel distributors.

Integration of Systems Biology for Agricultural Applications

Overview

Systems biology is an interdisciplinary field that focuses on complex interactions within biological systems. In agriculture, it applies computational models, data analysis, and holistic approaches to enhance crop productivity, improve resilience, and develop sustainable practices. By integrating systems biology, agricultural scientists can gain insights into plant biology, environmental interactions, and agricultural processes.

Key Components of Systems Biology in Agriculture

Genomics:

Definition: The study of an organism's complete set of DNA, including all of its genes.

Application: Identifying and characterizing genes responsible for traits such as drought tolerance, pest resistance, and nutrient use efficiency.

Transcriptomics:

Definition: The analysis of gene expression patterns.

Application: Understanding how plants respond to environmental stressors at the gene expression level, allowing for the identification of stress-responsive genes.

Proteomics:

Definition: The study of the structure and function of proteins produced by a genome.

Application: Investigating how proteins interact during plant growth and stress responses, helping to discover biomarkers for plant health.

Metabolomics:

Definition: The comprehensive analysis of metabolites within a biological sample.

Application: Profiling metabolic changes in plants under different conditions (e.g., nutrient deficiencies or pathogen attacks) to identify key metabolic pathways.

Environmental Interactions:

Definition: Understanding how plants interact with their environment.

Application: Studying soil microbiomes, plant-microbe interactions, and climatic factors to optimize growth conditions and improve yield.

Applications in Agriculture

Crop Improvement:

Example: Using genomics and metabolomics to develop crops with enhanced traits, such as increased yield or improved nutritional value.

Outcome: Accelerated breeding programs leading to faster development of improved crop varieties.

Stress Resistance:

Example: Identifying genetic markers associated with drought tolerance using transcriptomics.

Outcome: Development of crops that can withstand water scarcity, thereby ensuring food security.

Sustainable Practices:

Example: Understanding nutrient cycling in soil ecosystems through systems biology approaches.

Outcome: Implementation of precision agriculture practices that minimize fertilizer use while maximizing crop output.

Pest and Disease Management:

Example: Analyzing plant responses to pathogens using proteomics.

Outcome: Development of resistant crop varieties and targeted pest management strategies.

Resource Use Efficiency:

Example: Employing systems biology to optimize water and nutrient uptake in plants.

Outcome: Improved resource efficiency, reduced input costs, and environmental impact.

Case Study: Integrated Pest Management (IPM)

Background: Integrated Pest Management combines biological, cultural, physical, and chemical tools to manage pests sustainably.

Implementation:

Systems Biology Approach:

Data Integration: Using genomic, proteomic, and metabolomic data to understand plant-pest interactions.

Modeling: Creating predictive models to assess pest population dynamics and crop response.

Outcome:

Enhanced Decision-Making: Improved timing and methods for pest control, reducing pesticide use while maintaining crop yields.

Sustainability: Increased use of natural pest control methods, promoting biodiversity and reducing chemical inputs.

Biosensor Development in Agricultural Management

Overview

Biosensors are analytical devices that combine a biological component with a physicochemical detector to monitor biological processes. In agricultural management, biosensors are used to enhance crop production, monitor soil health, detect pests, and ensure food safety. They enable real-time data collection and analysis, facilitating informed decision-making and efficient resource management.

Key Components of Agricultural Biosensors

Bioreceptor:

This is the biological element that interacts with the target analyte (e.g., pathogens, nutrients). Common bioreceptors include enzymes, antibodies, nucleic acids, and microbial cells.

Transducer:

Converts the biological response into a measurable signal (electrical, optical, or thermal). The choice of transducer depends on the specific application and the type of biosensor being developed.

Signal Processing Unit:

Processes the signal generated by the transducer and converts it into a readable output, often using software for data analysis.

Display Unit:

Presents the data to the user in a comprehensible format, such as graphs, numbers, or alerts.

Applications of Biosensors in Agriculture

Soil Monitoring:

Nutrient Detection: Biosensors can detect soil nutrients like nitrogen, phosphorus, and potassium in real-time. This helps farmers optimize fertilization practices, reducing waste and enhancing crop yield.

pH Monitoring: Regular monitoring of soil pH ensures optimal conditions for plant growth.

Crop Health Assessment:

Disease Detection: Biosensors can identify specific pathogens or toxins in plants, enabling early detection of diseases and timely intervention.

Stress Monitoring: Sensors that measure plant responses to environmental stress (e.g., drought, salinity) can provide insights into crop health and resilience.

Pest Management:

Pest Detection: Biosensors can be designed to detect specific insect pests or their pheromones, allowing for targeted pest management strategies that minimize pesticide use.

Microbial Detection: Monitoring for harmful bacteria or fungi in crops can prevent crop losses and ensure food safety.

Water Quality Monitoring:

Irrigation Management: Biosensors can assess the quality of irrigation water, detecting contaminants or pathogens that may affect crop health.

Food Safety:

Contaminant Detection: Biosensors can test for pesticide residues, heavy metals, or pathogens in food products, ensuring safety for consumers.

Traceability: Using biosensors to monitor food quality during production and distribution enhances traceability and compliance with safety standards.

Case Studies

1. Soil Nutrient Biosensors

Background: A research project aimed at developing biosensors for real-time monitoring of soil nutrients.

Implementation:

Bioreceptor: Enzymes that react with specific nutrients (e.g., urease for nitrogen).

Transducer: Electrochemical sensors that measure changes in electrical signals based on enzyme activity.

Outcome:

Farmers using these biosensors were able to reduce fertilizer application by 30% while maintaining crop yield, leading to cost savings and reduced environmental impact.

2. Disease Detection in Crops

Background: A biosensor designed to detect specific plant pathogens, such as Pseudomonas syringae, responsible for leaf spot diseases.

Implementation:

Bioreceptor: Antibodies specific to the pathogen.

Transducer: Optical sensors that detect changes in light absorption when the antibody binds to the pathogen.

Outcome:

Early detection allowed farmers to implement targeted treatments, reducing disease spread and crop loss by 50%.

Challenges in Biosensor Development

Specificity and Sensitivity:

Ensuring that biosensors can accurately detect low concentrations of target analytes while avoiding interference from other substances.

Field Durability:

Developing biosensors that can withstand harsh environmental conditions (temperature fluctuations, humidity, etc.).

Cost:

Reducing the production costs of biosensors to make them affordable for farmers, especially smallholders.

Data Management:

Integrating biosensor data into existing agricultural management systems for effective decision-making.

Future Directions

Integration with IoT:

Combining biosensors with Internet of Things (IoT) technology for real-time monitoring and remote management of agricultural practices.

User-Friendly Design:

Developing biosensors that are easy to use, requiring minimal training for farmers to operate effectively.

Multi-Analyte Sensors:

Creating sensors capable of detecting multiple parameters simultaneously (e.g., soil moisture, nutrient levels) to provide comprehensive data.

Sustainability:

Focusing on eco-friendly materials and methods in biosensor design to align with sustainable agricultural practices.

V

ENTREPRENEURSHIP OPPORTUNITY IN INDUSTRIAL BIOTECHNOLOGY

Bioentrepreneurship involves creating and managing businesses in the biotechnology sector, focusing on developing products and services that utilize biological resources. With advancements in technology and increasing awareness of sustainability, bioentrepreneurship offers numerous opportunities across various fields, including agriculture, healthcare, environmental management, and food production.

Business Opportunities

a. Biotechnology in Agriculture

Opportunities: Development of genetically modified organisms (GMOs), biofertilizers, biopesticides, and sustainable farming techniques.

Market Demand: Growing need for food security and sustainable agricultural practices.

b. Healthcare and Pharmaceuticals

Opportunities: Development of biopharmaceuticals, diagnostics, and personalized medicine solutions.

Market Demand: Increasing prevalence of chronic diseases and demand for innovative treatments.

c. Environmental Biotechnology

Opportunities: Bioremediation technologies, waste management solutions, and sustainable energy (e.g., biofuels).

Market Demand: Rising concerns about pollution and climate change.

d. Food Biotechnology

Opportunities: Production of functional foods, nutraceuticals, and plant-based alternatives.

Market Demand: Consumer trends toward health and wellness products.

Essential Requirements

a. Research and Development (R&D)

Investment in R&D: Essential for developing innovative biotechnological products and services.

Collaboration: Partnerships with universities and research institutions can enhance R&D efforts.

b. Skilled Workforce

Talent Acquisition: Recruit scientists, researchers, and technicians with expertise in biotechnology.

Training Programs: Continuous training and development to keep staff updated on industry trends and technologies.

c. Regulatory Compliance

Understanding Regulations: Knowledge of biotechnology regulations and standards (e.g., FDA, EPA) is crucial for product development and marketing.

Documentation: Proper documentation and processes to meet regulatory requirements.

d. Funding and Investment

Initial Capital: Securing funding through venture capital, government grants, or angel investors to support business development.

Financial Management: Effective budgeting and financial planning to ensure sustainable growth.

Marketing Strategies

a. Identifying Target Markets

Market Segmentation: Understand and identify specific target markets for biotechnology products (e.g., farmers for biopesticides, healthcare providers for biopharmaceuticals).

Consumer Education: Educating consumers about the benefits of biotechnology and its applications.

b. Branding and Positioning

Brand Development: Create a strong brand identity that communicates quality, safety, and sustainability.

Differentiation: Highlight unique features of products, such as eco-friendliness, effectiveness, and scientific backing.

c. Digital Marketing

Online Presence: Utilize websites, social media, and content marketing to reach potential customers and stakeholders.

SEO and Content Strategy: Optimize online content for search engines to attract organic traffic and educate customers.

d. Networking and Partnerships

Industry Conferences: Attend biotechnology conferences and trade shows to connect with potential partners and clients.

Collaborations: Form alliances with research institutions, NGOs, and government bodies for joint projects and initiatives.

4. Schemes and Initiatives

a. Government Support Programs

Grants and Subsidies: Many governments provide funding opportunities and incentives for biotech startups focusing on research and innovation.

Accelerator Programs: Joining biotechnology incubators or accelerators can provide mentorship, resources, and funding access.

b. Public-Private Partnerships

Collaboration with Government: Engaging in partnerships with government agencies can enhance credibility and support for business initiatives.

Research Collaborations: Partnering with universities for joint research projects can lead to innovative product development.

c. Eco-Innovation Initiatives

Sustainability Schemes: Participating in eco-innovation programs can help companies develop environmentally friendly products while gaining access to funding and support.

Challenges and Scope in Pollution Monitoring and Bioremediation

Pollution monitoring and bioremediation for industrial pollutants, pesticides, and herbicides are critical areas in environmental management. While these sectors present significant opportunities, they also come with various challenges that need to be addressed for effective implementation and sustainability.

Challenges

Technical Challenges

Complexity of Pollutants: Industrial pollutants can vary widely in chemical structure, toxicity, and persistence in the environment, complicating the development of effective monitoring and bioremediation strategies.

Bioremediation Efficacy: Not all pollutants are easily biodegradable. Some toxic compounds may inhibit the activity of microorganisms used in bioremediation.

Regulatory Challenges

Compliance with Regulations: Navigating environmental regulations and obtaining necessary permits can be time-consuming and complex.

Monitoring Standards: Variability in pollution monitoring standards across regions can complicate compliance for businesses operating in multiple jurisdictions.

Economic Challenges

High Initial Costs: Setting up pollution monitoring systems and bioremediation projects can require significant upfront investment, which may deter smaller companies.

Uncertain ROI: The long-term financial benefits of bioremediation projects can be uncertain, making it difficult for companies to justify investments.

Public Awareness and Acceptance

Perception Issues: There can be skepticism about the effectiveness of bioremediation techniques, especially if past projects have failed.

Community Engagement: Engaging local communities and stakeholders is crucial for the success of bioremediation projects, but it can be challenging.

Data Management

Real-time Data Analysis: Collecting and analyzing large amounts of environmental data requires robust systems and technology, which may be lacking in some areas.

Integration with Existing Systems: Ensuring that new monitoring technologies integrate smoothly with existing environmental management systems can be difficult.

Scope of Pollution Monitoring and Bioremediation

Market Demand

With increasing industrialization and environmental awareness, the demand for effective pollution monitoring and remediation solutions is growing. Governments and industries are seeking sustainable practices to minimize environmental impact.

Technological Advancements

Advances in biotechnology, remote sensing, and data analytics are paving the way for more effective pollution monitoring and bioremediation strategies. This includes the development of biosensors, drones for remote monitoring, and improved bioremediation techniques.

Regulatory Support

Governments worldwide are implementing stricter environmental regulations, creating a favorable environment for businesses focused on pollution monitoring and remediation. This regulatory push can lead to increased funding and support for innovative solutions.

Sustainability Initiatives

Companies are increasingly recognizing the importance of sustainability, leading to more investments in green technologies and practices. This trend opens new avenues for businesses specializing in eco-friendly pollution control.

Public Awareness and Advocacy

Growing public awareness and advocacy for environmental protection are driving demand for effective pollution monitoring and bioremediation solutions. Community engagement and education can enhance project acceptance and support.

Case Study: Pollution Monitoring and Bioremediation for Industrial Pollutants

Company Overview: EcoRestore Technologies is a startup focusing on pollution monitoring and bioremediation solutions for industrial sites contaminated with heavy metals and organic pollutants.

Project Overview: The company undertook a project at a former manufacturing site known for soil and groundwater contamination due to heavy metal discharge and pesticide residues.

Implementation Steps:

Pollution Monitoring:

Technology Used: EcoRestore deployed a network of real-time sensors to monitor soil and groundwater quality, specifically targeting heavy metals (e.g., lead, cadmium) and pesticide levels.

Data Collection: The collected data was analyzed to identify pollution hotspots and assess the extent of contamination.

Bioremediation Strategy:

Phytoremediation: The company utilized hyperaccumulator plants (e.g., Indian mustard) known for their ability to absorb heavy metals from the soil.

Bioaugmentation: Specific strains of bacteria were introduced to the site to degrade organic pollutants, including pesticides.

Community Engagement:

EcoRestore conducted workshops to educate the local community about the bioremediation process, its benefits, and the importance of environmental protection.

Collaborated with local authorities to ensure compliance with regulatory requirements and gain community support.

Results:

Pollution Reduction: Within two years, EcoRestore achieved a 60% reduction in heavy metal concentration in the soil and significant degradation of pesticide residues.

Economic Benefits: The project not only restored the land but also increased property values in the surrounding area, attracting new businesses and residents.

Positive Community Impact: Community awareness and support for environmental initiatives increased, leading to further collaboration on local sustainability projects.

Conclusion

Pollution monitoring and bioremediation present significant challenges but also vast opportunities for innovation and sustainability. By addressing technical, regulatory, and economic challenges while leveraging technological advancements and community engagement, businesses can effectively navigate this landscape. The case study of EcoRestore Technologies illustrates the potential for successful implementation of these strategies, benefiting both the environment and local communities. As awareness of environmental issues continues to grow, the scope for pollution monitoring and bioremediation will only expand, making it a critical area for future investment and development.

Integrated Compost Production: Microbe-Enriched Compost

Integrated compost production, particularly microbe-enriched compost, is a sustainable approach to waste management and soil fertility enhancement. This process utilizes organic waste materials and beneficial microorganisms to produce high-quality compost that improves soil health and plant growth.

Microbe-Enriched Compost

Microbe-enriched compost is a type of compost that incorporates a diverse population of beneficial microorganisms, including bacteria, fungi, and actinomycetes, which play crucial roles in decomposing organic matter and enhancing soil health. This composting method aims to create a nutrient-rich soil amendment that promotes healthy plant growth and sustainable agriculture.

Importance of Microbe-Enriched Compost

Nutrient Availability: Microorganisms help break down organic matter into nutrients (nitrogen, phosphorus, potassium) that are readily available to plants.

Soil Structure Improvement: The microbial activity enhances soil aggregation, improving water retention and aeration.

Disease Suppression: Beneficial microbes can inhibit the growth of soil-borne pathogens, reducing plant diseases.

Sustainable Waste Management: Composting organic waste reduces landfill burden and contributes to a circular economy.

Integrated Compost Production Process

A. Feedstock Selection

Types of Organic Waste:

Kitchen scraps (vegetable and fruit peels)

Yard waste (leaves, grass clippings, small branches)

Agricultural residues (crop residues, manure)

Avoid:

Meat, dairy, and oils, as they can attract pests and create odors.

B. Preparation of Materials

Shredding:

Shred or chop larger materials to increase surface area and accelerate decomposition.

Mixing:

Combine carbon-rich (browns, e.g., dry leaves, straw) and nitrogen-rich (greens, e.g., fresh grass clippings, food scraps) materials in a balanced ratio (typically around 30:1 carbon to nitrogen).

C. Inoculation with Microorganisms

Microbial Sources:

Use commercially available microbial inoculants or introduce natural sources like mature compost, vermicompost, or soil to enhance microbial diversity.

Application:

Mix the inoculants evenly throughout the compost pile to ensure uniform distribution of microbes.

D. Composting Process

Composting Methods:

Aerobic Composting: Pile compost in an open bin or heap, allowing oxygen flow, promoting aerobic microbes that efficiently decompose materials.

Anaerobic Composting: In sealed environments (e.g., Bokashi), anaerobic microbes are utilized to ferment materials. This method requires less space but may have a slower decomposition rate.

Temperature Management:

Monitor temperatures to maintain them between 130°F to 160°F (54°C to 71°C) for effective decomposition. Turn the pile every few weeks to aerate and regulate temperature.

E. Curing and Maturation

Curing Phase:

After the active composting phase, allow the compost to cure for several weeks to months. This phase enables the remaining organic matter to fully decompose and microbial activity to stabilize.

Indicators of Maturity:

The compost should have a dark brown color, crumbly texture, and earthy smell. No identifiable materials should remain.

4. Application of Microbe-Enriched Compost

Soil Amendment: Incorporate compost into garden beds, lawns, or agricultural fields to improve soil fertility and structure.

Seed Starting Mix: Use compost as part of a seed starting mix to provide essential nutrients and beneficial microbes for young plants.

Mulching: Spread a layer of compost on the soil surface to suppress weeds, retain moisture, and gradually release nutrients.

5. Benefits of Microbe-Enriched Compost

Enhanced Soil Fertility: Provides a rich source of nutrients for plants, reducing the need for chemical fertilizers.

Improved Soil Health: Increases microbial diversity in the soil, promoting a healthy ecosystem that supports plant growth.

Environmental Benefits: Reduces organic waste in landfills, lowers greenhouse gas emissions, and fosters sustainable agricultural practices.

Bio Pesticide Production

Bio pesticides, or bio insecticides, are natural organisms or substances derived from natural sources that are used to control pests, diseases, and weeds. Unlike synthetic chemical pesticides, bio pesticides are generally less harmful to the environment, human health, and non-target organisms. They can be made from various biological sources, including plants, bacteria, fungi, and minerals.

1. Types of Bio Pesticides

Microbial Pesticides:

Definition: Contain microorganisms (bacteria, fungi, viruses) that target specific pests.

Examples:

Bacillus thuringiensis (Bt): A bacterium that produces toxins harmful to caterpillars and other insect larvae.

Beauveria bassiana: A fungus that infects and kills various insect pests.

Plant-Incorporated Protectants (PIPs):

Definition: Genetically engineered plants that produce their own bio pesticide compounds.

Example: Plants engineered to express Bt toxins, providing protection against certain insects.

Natural Products:

Definition: Extracts or oils derived from plants or other natural sources that deter or kill pests.

Examples:

Neem oil: Extracted from the seeds of the neem tree (Azadirachta indica), effective against a range of pests.

Pyrethrins: Derived from chrysanthemum flowers, known for their insecticidal properties.

Biochemical Pesticides:

Definition: Naturally occurring substances that disrupt pest behavior.

Examples:

Insect growth regulators (IGRs): Substances that interfere with the development of insects.

Pheromones: Chemicals released by insects to attract mates, which can be used in traps to control populations.

2. *Production Process of Bio Pesticides*

A. Selection of Raw Materials

Microbial Sources:

Identify beneficial microorganisms suitable for pest control (e.g., Bacillus thuringiensis, Beauveria bassiana).

Source from natural environments, laboratories, or commercial suppliers.

Plant Materials:

Select plants known for their pesticidal properties (e.g., neem, garlic, chrysanthemum).

Ensure materials are free from contaminants and disease.

B. Cultivation of Microorganisms

Inoculum Preparation:

Grow selected microorganisms in a laboratory setting using appropriate growth media (e.g., nutrient broth for bacteria or specific substrates for fungi).

Maintain optimal conditions (temperature, pH, aeration) for growth.

Harvesting:

Once the microorganisms reach the desired density, harvest them using centrifugation or filtration methods.

C. Extraction of Plant Compounds

Extraction Methods:

Use methods like cold pressing, solvent extraction, or steam distillation to extract active compounds from plant materials.

Select solvents (e.g., ethanol, methanol, or water) based on the solubility of the target compounds.

Purification:

Purify the extracts using techniques such as chromatography to isolate active ingredients.

D. Formulation

Formulating the Bio Pesticide:

Combine the harvested microorganisms or extracted plant compounds with carriers, adjuvants, or stabilizers to enhance efficacy and shelf-life.

Common formulations include powders, granules, emulsifiable concentrates, or ready-to-use sprays.

Testing for Efficacy:

Conduct laboratory and field tests to evaluate the bio pesticide's effectiveness against target pests.

Adjust formulations based on test results for optimal performance.

E. Packaging and Labeling

Packaging:

Package the final product in suitable containers to protect it from moisture, light, and contamination.

Ensure packaging materials are environmentally friendly and recyclable.

Labeling:

Label products clearly, providing information on usage instructions, safety precautions, active ingredients, and environmental considerations.

3. Advantages of Bio Pesticides

Environmental Safety: Generally less harmful to non-target species, including beneficial insects, wildlife, and humans.

Sustainability: Often derived from renewable resources, contributing to sustainable agricultural practices.

Resistance Management: Help manage resistance in pest populations when used in rotation with synthetic pesticides.

Health Benefits: Lower risk of pesticide residues on food, contributing to food safety and public health.

4. Challenges in Bio Pesticide Production

Regulatory Hurdles: Navigating the regulatory landscape for approval can be complex and time-consuming, varying by region.

Stability and Shelf Life: Bio pesticides may have shorter shelf lives compared to synthetic options, requiring careful formulation and storage conditions.

Market Acceptance: There can be skepticism about the effectiveness of bio pesticides among farmers used to conventional methods.

Efficacy Variability: The effectiveness of bio pesticides can vary based on environmental conditions, pest species, and application methods.

Fermented Products: Probiotics and Prebiotics

Fermented products are foods and beverages created through the process of fermentation, where microorganisms such as bacteria, yeast, or molds convert sugars and starches into acids, gases, or alcohol. This process not only preserves food but also enhances its nutritional profile. Within the realm of fermented products, probiotics and prebiotics play essential roles in promoting gut health and overall wellness.

1. Probiotics

Definition: Probiotics are live microorganisms that, when consumed in adequate amounts, confer health benefits to the host, primarily by improving or restoring gut flora.

A. Sources of Probiotics

Dairy Products:

Yogurt: Contains live cultures of beneficial bacteria like Lactobacillus and Bifidobacterium.

Kefir: A fermented milk drink containing a diverse range of probiotic strains.

Fermented Vegetables:

Sauerkraut: Fermented cabbage rich in Lactobacillus bacteria.

Kimchi: A Korean dish made from fermented vegetables, typically including cabbage and radishes.

Other Sources:

Kombucha: A fermented tea that contains various strains of bacteria and yeast.

Miso: A fermented soybean paste used in Japanese cuisine.

Tempeh: A fermented soybean product that provides protein and probiotics.

B. Health Benefits

Gut Health: Probiotics help balance the gut microbiome, aiding digestion and preventing gastrointestinal disorders such as diarrhea and irritable bowel syndrome (IBS).

Immune Support: They can enhance immune function and help the body fend off infections.

Mental Health: Emerging research suggests a connection between gut health and mental well-being, with probiotics potentially alleviating symptoms of anxiety and depression.

Nutrient Absorption: Probiotics can improve the absorption of essential nutrients, including vitamins and minerals.

2. *Prebiotics*

Definition: Prebiotics are non-digestible fibers and compounds that promote the growth and activity of beneficial bacteria in the gut. Unlike probiotics, they are not live organisms.

A. Sources of Prebiotics

Fruits and Vegetables:

Bananas: Rich in fructooligosaccharides (FOS).

Onions and Garlic: Contain inulin, a type of prebiotic fiber.

Whole Grains:

Oats and Barley: Provide beta-glucans and other soluble fibers that act as prebiotics.

Legumes:

Beans, lentils, and chickpeas are excellent sources of prebiotic fibers.

Other Sources:

Asparagus and artichokes: High in inulin and other fermentable fibers.

B. Health Benefits

Gut Microbiome Support: Prebiotics serve as food for probiotics, enhancing their growth and activity in the gut.

Improved Digestion: They help increase stool frequency and improve overall digestive health.

Enhanced Mineral Absorption: Prebiotics can enhance the absorption of minerals such as calcium and magnesium, supporting bone health.

Blood Sugar Regulation: Some studies suggest that prebiotics may help regulate blood sugar levels and improve insulin sensitivity.

3. The Synergy Between Probiotics and Prebiotics

Synbiotics: The combination of probiotics and prebiotics in the same product is termed a synbiotic. This synergy maximizes the benefits for gut health. Prebiotics serve as a food source for probiotics, enhancing their survival and colonization in the gut.

Applications: Many fermented products, such as yogurt with added fiber, are designed to deliver both probiotics and prebiotics, promoting a balanced gut microbiome.

Stem Cell Production, Stem Cell Bank, and Contract Research

Stem cells are undifferentiated cells with the potential to develop into various cell types. They are pivotal in regenerative medicine, therapeutic applications, and research. Stem cell production involves obtaining and cultivating these cells, while stem cell banks store them for future use. Contract research organizations (CROs) provide research services to support stem cell research and development.

1. Stem Cell Production

A. Types of Stem Cells

Embryonic Stem Cells (ESCs):

Derived from early-stage embryos (blastocysts).

Pluripotent, meaning they can differentiate into nearly any cell type in the body.

Adult Stem Cells (Somatic Stem Cells):

Found in various tissues (e.g., bone marrow, blood, adipose tissue).

Multipotent, meaning they can differentiate into a limited range of cell types related to their tissue of origin.

Induced Pluripotent Stem Cells (iPSCs):

Adult cells reprogrammed to an embryonic-like state through genetic modification.

Pluripotent and can differentiate into various cell types.

B. Production Process

Isolation:

For ESCs, embryos are created via in vitro fertilization and then cultured to obtain stem cells.

For adult stem cells, tissues are harvested (e.g., bone marrow aspiration).

Cultivation:

Stem cells are cultured in specialized media under controlled conditions to promote growth and maintain pluripotency or multipotency.

Conditions include appropriate temperature, oxygen levels, and nutrient supply.

Characterization:

Stem cells must be characterized to confirm their type and potency through various assays (e.g., surface marker analysis, differentiation assays).

2. Stem Cell Bank

A. Purpose of Stem Cell Banks

Stem cell banks collect, process, and store stem cells for future use in research, therapy, or transplantation. They ensure the availability of high-quality stem cells for clinical and research applications.

B. Types of Stem Cell Banks

Public Stem Cell Banks:

Provide free access to stem cell lines for research and therapy.

Funded by governmental or non-profit organizations.

Private Stem Cell Banks:

Offer services to individuals or families, allowing them to store their own stem cells (e.g., cord blood) for personal use.

Typically charge fees for collection, processing, and storage.

C. Operations

Collection:

Collection protocols must comply with ethical standards and regulations.

Examples include cord blood collection at birth or bone marrow aspiration.

Processing:

Stem cells are processed to isolate and purify the desired cell population.

This may involve cryopreservation to maintain cell viability.

Storage:

Stem cells are stored in liquid nitrogen tanks at ultra-low temperatures to preserve their functionality for future use.

3. Contract Research Organizations (CROs)

A. Role of CROs in Stem Cell Research

CROs provide outsourced research services to pharmaceutical, biotechnology, and academic institutions. They help accelerate the development of stem cell-based therapies and products.

B. Services Offered by CROs

Preclinical Research:

Conduct studies to evaluate the safety and efficacy of stem cell therapies.

Includes in vitro testing, animal studies, and pharmacokinetic evaluations.

Clinical Trials:

Assist in designing, implementing, and managing clinical trials for stem cell therapies.

Ensure compliance with regulatory standards and ethical guidelines.

Regulatory Support:

Help navigate the regulatory landscape for stem cell products, including preparing documentation for regulatory submissions (e.g., IND applications).

Manufacturing Support:

Provide facilities and expertise for the large-scale production of stem cells and related products, ensuring quality and consistency.

Production of Monoclonal and Polyclonal Antibodies

Antibodies are proteins produced by the immune system to identify and neutralize foreign objects like bacteria and viruses. They can be categorized into monoclonal and polyclonal antibodies, each with distinct production methods, characteristics, and applications.

1. Monoclonal Antibodies

Definition: Monoclonal antibodies (mAbs) are identical antibodies produced from a single clone of B cells. They are specific to a particular antigen and are widely used in diagnostics, therapeutics, and research.

A. Production Process

Immunization:

Mice (commonly used) are immunized with a specific antigen (e.g., a protein from a pathogen).

Booster shots are often given to enhance the immune response.

Cell Fusion:

Spleen cells from the immunized mouse, which produce the desired antibodies, are isolated.

These B cells are fused with myeloma cells (cancerous B cells) to create hybridoma cells.

The fusion is facilitated by polyethylene glycol (PEG) or electric fields.

Selection of Hybridomas:

The resulting hybridomas are cultured in a selective medium (e.g., HAT medium) that allows only hybridoma cells to survive.

Screening is performed to identify hybridomas producing the desired antibody using techniques like enzyme-linked immunosorbent assay (ELISA).

Cloning and Expansion:

Selected hybridomas are cloned to produce identical cells.

The cloned cells are expanded in culture to produce large quantities of the specific monoclonal antibody.

Purification:

The antibodies are harvested from the culture supernatant.

Techniques such as protein A affinity chromatography or ion-exchange chromatography are used for purification.

Characterization:

The purified monoclonal antibodies are characterized for specificity, affinity, and purity through assays like Western blotting or flow cytometry.

2. Polyclonal Antibodies

Definition: Polyclonal antibodies are a mixture of antibodies produced by different B cell clones in response to a specific antigen. They recognize multiple epitopes on the same antigen.

A. Production Process

Immunization:

Animals (e.g., rabbits, goats, or sheep) are immunized with the target antigen.

Multiple doses may be administered to boost the immune response.

Serum Collection:

After a defined period, blood is drawn from the immunized animal.

Serum is collected, which contains a diverse array of antibodies against the antigen.

Purification (Optional):

The antibodies can be purified from serum using techniques like ammonium sulfate precipitation or affinity chromatography.

However, many applications use the unpurified serum, which contains a mixture of antibodies.

Characterization:

The antibody response can be assessed using methods like ELISA or Western blotting to determine the titer and specificity.

3. Applications

Monoclonal Antibodies:

Diagnostics: Used in tests like ELISA, Western blotting, and immunohistochemistry.

Therapeutics: Employed in cancer treatment, autoimmune diseases, and infectious diseases (e.g., trastuzumab for breast cancer).

Research: Tools for studying specific proteins, cell types, and pathways.

Polyclonal Antibodies:

Diagnostics: Commonly used in assays and detection methods (e.g., pregnancy tests, various ELISAs).

Research: Useful in various applications, including Western blotting and immunoprecipitation, where recognizing multiple epitopes can improve signal strength and detection.

4. Advantages and Disadvantages

Monoclonal Antibodies:

Advantages: Highly specific to one epitope, consistent in production, and can be produced in large quantities.

Disadvantages: More expensive to produce and require complex technologies.

Polyclonal Antibodies:

Advantages: Easier and cheaper to produce, can recognize multiple epitopes, which can enhance detection.

Disadvantages: Batch-to-batch variability and potential cross-reactivity with non-target antigens.

Single Cell Protein and Secondary Metabolite Production

Single Cell Protein (SCP) refers to the protein extracted from microorganisms such as bacteria, yeast, and fungi. It serves as a protein supplement in animal feed and human diets. Secondary metabolites are organic compounds produced by organisms that are not directly involved in their growth or reproduction, often playing crucial roles in ecological interactions, such as defense and signaling.

1. Single Cell Protein (SCP)

Definition: SCP is defined as the protein derived from the microbial biomass of unicellular organisms that can be used as a nutritional supplement.

A. Sources of SCP

Yeast: Saccharomyces cerevisiae (brewer's yeast) and Candida utilis.

Fungi: Filamentous fungi such as Fusarium and Aspergillus species.

Bacteria: Species like Methylophilus methylotrophus and Corynebacterium.

B. Production Process

Fermentation:

Microorganisms are cultured in a bioreactor using various substrates (e.g., molasses, agricultural residues, or waste materials) under controlled conditions.

Conditions like pH, temperature, and aeration are optimized for maximum growth and protein yield.

Harvesting:

After fermentation, the microbial biomass is harvested through centrifugation or filtration.

The moisture content is reduced, often through drying methods such as spray drying or freeze-drying.

Processing:

The harvested biomass may be further processed to improve flavor, texture, or digestibility.

It can be blended with other food components to enhance nutritional value.

C. Nutritional Aspects

SCP is rich in protein (up to 70% dry weight), vitamins, and essential amino acids.

It is often used in animal feed formulations, aquaculture, and as a supplement in human food (e.g., protein bars and shakes).

D. Advantages

SCP production utilizes low-cost substrates, including agricultural waste and by-products.

It has a lower environmental footprint compared to traditional animal protein sources.

2. Secondary Metabolite Production

Definition: Secondary metabolites are compounds produced by microorganisms that are not essential for basic metabolic processes but have important ecological functions and applications.

A. Types of Secondary Metabolites

Antibiotics: E.g., penicillin, produced by Penicillium fungi.

Alkaloids: E.g., morphine from the opium poppy (Papaver somniferum).

Flavonoids: Plant-derived compounds with antioxidant properties.

Terpenes: Compounds like menthol and limonene that contribute to flavor and aroma.

B. Production Process

Microbial Fermentation:

Specific strains of bacteria, fungi, or plants are cultured under conditions that promote secondary metabolite production, typically during the stationary phase of growth.

Conditions such as nutrient limitation, stress (e.g., pH changes, temperature), or the addition of precursors can enhance production.

Extraction:

Secondary metabolites are extracted from the biomass using solvents (e.g., ethanol, methanol) or through non-solvent methods like steam distillation.

The extraction process may involve filtering, concentrating, and purifying the compounds.

Characterization:

The extracted metabolites are characterized using techniques like chromatography, mass spectrometry, and nuclear magnetic resonance (NMR) spectroscopy to determine their structure and purity.

C. Applications

Pharmaceuticals: Many antibiotics and therapeutic agents are derived from secondary metabolites.

Agriculture: Some metabolites serve as biopesticides or herbicides, promoting sustainable agricultural practices.

Food Industry: Flavoring agents and preservatives derived from secondary metabolites are used in food products.

D. Advantages

Secondary metabolites often have unique properties that can lead to the development of novel drugs and agricultural products.

They are typically produced in small quantities, making their extraction and purification valuable for high-value applications.

Contract Research in Microbial Genomics

Contract research in microbial genomics involves outsourcing research and development activities related to the study of microbial genomes to specialized organizations. These organizations, known as Contract Research Organizations (CROs), provide a range of services that support genomic research in various fields, including healthcare, agriculture, and biotechnology.

1. Definition and Scope

Microbial Genomics: The study of the genomes of microorganisms, including bacteria, archaea, fungi, and viruses. This field involves sequencing, analyzing, and interpreting genomic data to understand microbial functions, diversity, and applications.

Contract Research: The practice of outsourcing research activities to specialized firms that have the expertise, technology, and resources to conduct genomic studies. This can include everything from sequencing to data analysis and interpretation.

2. Services Offered by CROs in Microbial Genomics

Genomic Sequencing:

High-throughput sequencing technologies (e.g., Illumina, PacBio) to determine the nucleotide sequence of microbial genomes.

Whole-genome sequencing (WGS) and targeted sequencing for specific genes or regions.

Bioinformatics Services:

Analysis of genomic data, including assembly, annotation, and comparative genomics.

Use of software tools to interpret genomic information and identify genes, regulatory elements, and pathways.

Metagenomics:

Study of genetic material recovered directly from environmental samples, allowing for the analysis of microbial communities without culturing.

Profiling of microbiomes in various environments (e.g., soil, water, human gut).

Functional Genomics:

Investigating the roles of genes in microbial metabolism and physiology.

Techniques such as gene knockout, overexpression, and RNA-seq to study gene function and expression levels.

Consulting and Regulatory Support:

Guidance on compliance with regulatory requirements for genomic research, especially in pharmaceuticals and food safety.

Assistance with study design, data management, and reporting.

3. Applications of Contract Research in Microbial Genomics

Healthcare and Pharmaceuticals:

Development of new antibiotics, vaccines, and diagnostics by understanding pathogenic microbial genomes.

Personalized medicine approaches based on the genomic profiles of pathogens.

Agriculture:

Improvement of crop resilience and productivity through the study of plant-associated microbes and their genomes.

Development of biopesticides and biofertilizers derived from beneficial microorganisms.

Environmental Biotechnology:

Bioremediation studies to utilize microbial genomics for the cleanup of polluted environments.

Monitoring and managing microbial diversity in ecosystems.

Food Industry:

Characterization of foodborne pathogens and fermentation microbes to ensure food safety and quality.

Development of probiotics and functional foods through understanding the microbiome.

4. Advantages of Contract Research in Microbial Genomics

Expertise: CROs typically have specialized knowledge and experience in microbial genomics, allowing for high-quality results.

Cost-Effectiveness: Outsourcing research can reduce costs associated with hiring in-house staff and maintaining laboratory facilities.

Access to Technology: CROs often possess advanced technologies and methodologies that may not be available internally.

Time Efficiency: CROs can expedite the research process, enabling faster project completion and quicker results.

Flexibility: Companies can engage CROs for specific projects without the long-term commitment of employing full-time staff.

Summary & Conclusion

Bioeconomy and Entrepreneurship delves into the rapidly evolving field of the bioeconomy, emphasizing its transformative role in reshaping industries and promoting sustainable development. The book outlines the foundations of the bioeconomy, explaining how biological resources, processes, and principles are becoming pivotal in creating value and addressing global environmental challenges. It explores various sectors, including agriculture, energy, healthcare, and waste management, where bio-based solutions are replacing traditional, often unsustainable, industrial practices.

The book also highlights how the bioeconomy opens unique entrepreneurial opportunities, with start-ups and companies leveraging biotechnology to drive innovation. Detailed case studies of successful bio-based enterprises illustrate how businesses can build economic value while prioritizing ecological sustainability. Furthermore, the book discusses policy frameworks, market trends, and investment avenues that support bio-innovation, providing a roadmap for entrepreneurs and stakeholders seeking to enter or expand within the bioeconomy.

The book concludes by underscoring the bioeconomy's potential to catalyze both economic growth and environmental stewardship. It argues that the future of sustainable development hinges on integrating bio-based practices across industries, where entrepreneurs and business leaders play a critical role. Ultimately, Bioeconomy and Entrepreneurship positions the bioeconomy not just as an industry but as a holistic approach to align economic ambitions with environmental responsibilities, inspiring a new wave of ventures committed to a greener, more resilient future.

www.ingramcontent.com/pod-product-compliance
Lightning Source LLC
LaVergne TN
LVHW091120150826
845673LV00002B/906

* 9 7 9 8 8 9 6 3 2 5 6 7 3 *